Dolina

AN ISLAND GIRL'S JOURNEY

Dolina Maclennan

In Conversation with
Jim Gilchrist and Stuart Eydmann

Islands Book Trust

LIVING HISTORY

THE ISLANDS BOOK TRUST
URRAS LEABHRAICHEAN NAN EILEAN

Published in 2014 by the Islands Book Trust

www.theislandsbooktrust.com

ISBN: 978-1-907443-61-9

Islands Book Trust, Laxay Hall, Laxay, Isle of Lewis, HS2 9PJ.
Tel: 01851 830316

Typeset by Erica Schwarz (www.schwarz-editorial.co.uk)
Cover design by Raspberry Creative Type
Printed and bound by Martins the Printers, Berwick upon Tweed

Unfortunately some of the images in this book are of poor quality; nevertheless these have been included because of their importance to the publication.

For my four wonderful girls: daughters Mary Brown and Jane Bechtel, and grand-daughters Catriona and Annie Bechtel – with all the love in the world

Contents

Contents

Introduction

THE genesis of this book lies in the launch party of another, a few years ago, toward the latter stages of which Doli was regaling Stuart Eydmann and me with some choice anecdotes from her eventful life. Stuart it was who suggested, perhaps unwisely, that somebody should be recording all this for the archive at the School of Scottish Studies. Our enthusiasms lubricated (and our better judgement perhaps a trifle dulled) by liberal quantities of book-launch wine, the three of us agreed that it should be done.

We started meeting at Doli's flat in Stockbridge, joined in the earliest stages of the project by her friend, the film producer Douglas Eadie. Initially at least, these recording sessions were unstructured, usually taking the form of often divertingly tangential conversations while going through Doli's myriad cardboard boxes of cuttings, correspondence, photographs and other memorabilia. These sessions were laced with often extraordinary anecdotes, much humour and not a few emotional moments.

While we embarked on this with no other thought in mind than to preserve these reminiscences of an interesting life, the idea of a book was hovering in the wings. Then Douglas, whose Pelicula Films is behind the long-running TV series 'The Transatlantic Sessions' and many documentaries, declared that he and director Mike Alexander wanted to make one on Doli's life. This they duly did, and the resulting hour-long programme, 'Dolina', was broadcast on BBC Alba on Ne'erday 2012 (Doli's 74th birthday).

With John Randall of the Islands Book Trust taking a keen (and very patient) interest, the imperative changed somewhat. We tried, not always successfully, to structure our interviews more, at the same time sifting through our earlier recorded interviews to arrange Doli's conversations for the printed page. At no point was this book envisaged as being 'ghost-written'. We stuck as closely as possible to her words, and, in fact, two of the chapters, that on her time with An Comunn Gàidhealach and the 'Bag Lady' episode were basically written by her.

The method we more or less fell into was to sort extracts from these recorded conversations into 'chapterettes', then read them over with Doli, who would make numerous changes and amendments. As a time-efficient way of writing a book, it is not to be recommended, although the lunches were delicious, as one might expect from the former proprietor of Blair Atholl's renowned Woodlands guest house.

As a book gradually took shape, it became clear what a remarkable life was being chronicled here, from a wartime childhood in a still strongly self-contained and essentially communal rural community in Lewis to the Howff and Waverley crucibles of the emergent Scottish folk revival; from school dramatics in Stornoway's Nicolson Institute to touring with 7:84's ground-breaking 'The Cheviot, the Stag and the Black, Black Oil' and a subsequent career in Gaelic broadcasting.

Collaborating with Doli in this has been a pleasure and, without resorting to cliché, a real privilege. And the soup and kedgeree were great.

Jim Gilchrist & Dr Stuart Eydmann
Edinburgh 2014

Preface

THIS is not an autobiography, so you can all relax. No tales out of school!

There are so many people, even within the boundaries of my own native village, whose journeys are much more remarkable and worthwhile than mine. There are captains of ships and of industry, ministers of religion, Queen Alexandra nurses, prisoners of war, survivors of shipwrecks, cowboys in Argentina, men of Hudson's Bay and of South Georgia. All those have or had a story to tell. It's a pity no-one thought to record them.

I was talked into recording my journey, and it has been quite an emotional three years, as memories surfaced, as I found photographs and letters and was reminded of things I would have preferred to forget. I'm sure we all have those.

This book would never have got past the talking stage without the dedication of Jim Gilchrist and Stuart Eydmann. How they coped with it all, and with my emotional moments, still baffles me, so thank you both. Thanks also to Pelicula Films and Douglas Eadie in particular, who was with Jim, Stuart and I for the first four months of reminiscing.

Further thanks to John MacInnes for his foreword and for being my friend for five decades; to Dòmhnall Uilleam Stiùbhart for keeping secrets; to my family for confirming stories, times and places; to John Herdman for his Heretics diaries; to all my family, friends, neighbours and acquaintances, past and present, who made my journey rich and worthwhile.

Finally thanks to John Randall of the Islands Book Trust for his patience, tolerance and faith in this project.

Dolina Maclennan

Foreword

---

*Dr John MacInnes, former lecturer at
the School of Scottish Studies*

DOLINA Maclennan's early childhood years were probably little different, at least in outline, from those of others who were monoglot Gaelic speakers until they entered school to be taught exclusively through the medium of English. Nonetheless, every family has its own characteristics and that is no doubt true of the Maclennans as well.

Dolina's father had spent some years in Canada before returning to his native Lewis, where he married a girl from the same island. Dolina remembers how he taught her brothers how to box, but it was not until adult life, during a visit to Canada, that she learned that 'Kid Maclennan' had been a noted boxer there, whose reputation was still vivid among his contemporaries. It is evident that there was a warm and affectionate bond between father and daughter, the youngest of the family, and that her father's death when she was still a young girl remains a poignant memory.

At secondary school in Stornoway Dolina studied Gaelic formally under a popular master, Alex Urquhart, from distant Ardnamurchan. Although that added a fresh dimension to her education it did not impair the distinctive intonation of her native speech. This is a remarkable survival which can be connected with certain dialects of Norwegian and is one of the legacies of Viking immigrants who settled in northern and western Scotland from around 800AD.

When Dolina came to work in Edinburgh in the 1950s, her exposition of traditional Gaelic song came as a revelation to audiences whose experience had hitherto been limited to that of Gaelic singing on the more fashionable public platforms of that time. Soon afterwards, she became a well-known presence on radio and television, and as a member of the celebrated 7:84 Theatre Company. These and other roles extended her fame throughout Scotland and Ireland and far beyond.

For those who know Gaelic, the drama series 'Na Moireasdanaich', 'The Morrisons', for which she wrote all the scripts, is without reservation one of the highlights of Dolina Maclennan's professional career. This sequence of naturalistic vignettes of the life of a crofting family was original and transformative in the development of Gaelic radio.

This memoir of an extraordinary creative output deserves to be widely read.

Chapter 1

The Last Little Fish in the Net

MY VERY earliest memory is of my cradle being given away. It had been made especially for me by Aonghas Lachie – Angus Smith, our neighbour at Number 19 – when I became a late addition to the family. I was sitting in it, it was mine, but it was being taken from me and, although I was small, I could feel the loss, a feeling I have had in many situations since. I remember everybody laughing, and being lifted out of the cradle and it being taken away. I suppose people weren't aware at that time of the delicacy of a child's sensibilities.

Another memory is that of my brother Duncan taking me to see grandmother Maclennan, and she giving me a halfpenny. It was written in the family Bible that she had died in 1941. I arrived in 1938, so I must have been about two and a half at the time. She was my father's mother, a Macmillan from Lemreway, and a close kinship still exists between the descendants of that family. My Maclennan grandfather, whom I never knew, had been in Canada with the Hudson Bay Company. He came back and built one of Marvig's first *taighean-geal* or white houses of mortared and rendered masonry and a slate, metal or bitumen roof rather than the traditional thatch. It was there that my uncle Donald, after whom I'm named, my father Angus, my uncle Alex Murdo and my aunties Christina and Peggy Ann were brought up.

Marvig is in the Lochs area of Lewis. My people had been part of the community since it was founded and I spent all my childhood there. I was the youngest by five years in a family of eight children, with five brothers and two sisters. The village of Marvig comprises twenty-four crofts and is located to the south of the mouth of Loch Erisort. It had its origins in the Park clearances when new holdings were established and settled with people from the area of Loch Shiel and Buthnish. They became greatly engaged in hand-line fishing which, until the last quarter of the nineteenth century, supported stations for curing and salting. When I was growing up there was still a disused *taigh-salluin* or salting-house by the shore beneath the school house. I believe that's where the men had 'the keg' for concerts and weddings.

My father's family croft, which ran right down to the water, was number 18 Marvig and was passed from my grandfather to Uncle Donald, his oldest son, who was a fisherman. It was a special place. All the land running down to the sea used to be richly covered in wild bluebells, with rowans and honeysuckle and primroses in all the nooks.

My father Angus Maclennan was a Hudson Bay man, like his father before him and like so many Lewis people and Orcadians. He became a trapper in his own right and came home from Canada and married my mother, but she would not go back there with him. However, he did go back to Canada, returning later to build the house just outside the village, bringing all the furniture from Edinburgh – beautiful, absolutely stunning pieces. It would be highly collectable now, but it was all thrown out when more modern furniture came in as it was 'just old rubbish'. The beautiful things were put in the byre, with sacks of oats stored in the cupboards and that sort of thing.

He also opened a shop beside the house and bought a horse and gig. By the time I was born the shop had closed. I think my mother gave credit to everybody. People were struggling. The horse was gone but the gig was still there. It was a beautiful thing, and I think my father gave away all its bits and pieces, the lanterns and all that, to the tinkers. He was great pals with them, the Drummonds especially, and the Stewarts, but I think it was the Drummonds who used to come round in the summer time with a horse and cart. In those days they were tinsmiths – that's where you bought your pails and your mugs. The tin mugs with the handle were called *mug a chèard*, tinkers' mugs. I mean, 'tinker' wasn't a derogatory term, and a *caird* is an artisan or smith. So the *cèaraidhean* were people who make things.

At the beginning of the war the shed that had been the shop was taken over. Two great big trucks came with sealed cardboard boxes, about a foot square, and they filled the shelves of what had been the shop, which was built as an addition to the house. We never knew what was in the boxes, whether it was emergency food or what, but they locked and sealed the door. The entrance gate to our road was narrow and they had to take the fence away to get the lorries up to the door of the shed. Then they came at the end of the war and took them all away again.

My father always regretted not settling permanently in Canada. He loved the place, but my mother didn't think she was good enough to live anywhere else. She thought everybody from 'away' was above her and that she was afraid that she wouldn't know how to behave properly. She was Mary Bell Mackenzie from

Croft 13. She had two brothers, Iain and Murdo and two sisters, Chirsty Ann (a herring net maker) and my Auntie Kate, who was the only one I knew. She had helped me into the world. Kate and her husband Alasdair (Mast) had ten of a family, including Murdani the famous village bard and songster.

Both my mother's father and her brother had tuberculosis and she was responsible for looking after them in their blackhouse until they died. Because they had tubercular wounds she used to have to pack them and burn the dressings. The doctor came from Keose by boat, because there were no roads, but he only came once in a blue moon. On one occasion when he visited he said she needed a holiday to get away from things, so he sent her to Shetland to gut herring – at sixteen. That was the only time she ever left Lewis until the 1970s, when she came to Aberdeenshire to stay with my sister Jessie and to visit me in Edinburgh. Her own mother had died when she was a child, and I remember her saying that she used to go out the back of the house alone and say to herself *"Mamaidh"*, just so that she could know what it was like to say that word. But she could be very funny: I remember after I had moved to Edinburgh I had taken her down the town and was showing her the place, and my husband George came home for his tea and he said, "How are you getting on Granny?" To which she replied, "Oh the bus conductors are very nice to me, but they know themselves I'm just a recruit." What a wonderful expression; we knew what she meant – green.

The oldest of my brothers was John Murdo, who died of rheumatic fever at the age of nine. I don't think my mother ever recovered from that loss. Although I wasn't yet born when he died, all my life I've been conscious of him as part of the family. People said of him that he had a special presence or aura, and I can still see that from the surviving picture of him. We were told that he died in the hospital singing the 103rd Psalm. The thought of this always made me cry and it still does. People said he was too good for this world, as they do when someone dies young.

He was followed by Duncan, then Christy Ann, Donald, Murdo, Jessie, then Murdie John, and then me in 1938; I was the *'isean deireadh linn',* 'the last little fish in the net' and obviously a mistake. My mother was forty-six and I was always aware that I wasn't expected. It might have been different had I been a boy. However, there I was.

My father doted on me. When he put me to bed he would lie down beside me and sing me *The Maple Leaf for Ever* or tell me stories about Canada and the things and places he knew and missed there. Fort William, Thunder Bay, Winnipeg ... I remember all those names because he used to talk of them every night. In Canada he had been an amateur boxing champion, as recorded in photographs. My cousin Ruth MacMillan visited Fort William (now known as Thunder Bay) and she stayed with the woman who had been my father's landlady, who said he would have been one of the richest men in Canada if he had come back. I remember when I was in Cape Breton Island in the early 1980s I met a group of fiddlers from Prince Edward Island who were doing a benefit concert for one of their musicians over near Antigonish, and there was this old, old man, probably aged about ninety. Something prompted me to say to him, "Have you ever heard of Kid Maclennan." He looked at me and said, "You mean with the hands?" My father had enormous hands. I was absolutely dumbfounded. Kid Maclennan; that's the name he fought under. And he said, "How do you know about Kid Maclennan?" I said, "He was my father." It was just amazing; he said there had been an article about the Hudson Bay pugilists in a magazine not so long ago which mentioned him. I don't know if boxing was encouraged but it was part of their culture. He taught all my brothers to box and there were half a dozen pairs of boxing gloves in the house.

Father was a diabetic, and I grew up thinking everybody's father had an injection before breakfast and before supper. He had to have to have a clean potty every morning – there was no bathroom and no electricity. There was a big marble-topped dresser on which stood a large bottle of blue liquid and syringes in methylated spirits in a glass bowl with a lid. We used to put about an inch of this blue stuff into a test tube, and we would put drops of his first morning urine into the tube and I would carry it through to the kitchen where there was a blackened syrup tin of water boiling on the open fire. I would put the tube into the boiling water and leave it for five minutes. The colour it changed to – clear blue or greeny-yellow – dictated his dosage of insulin for the day. The insulin was in little clear bottles with blue labels and black rubber tops, and from them he would load the syringe and inject himself. It was all glass, glass syringes and glass bowls and everything had to be sterile and his diet was very, very strict. We had to weigh everything. It was quite a palaver.

He died when he was fifty-eight. I was twelve and it had a terrible effect on me. I had gone to high school in Stornoway after I passed the 'Quali' – the Qualifying exam that was the equivalent of the Eleven-Plus. I only got home for one long weekend each term because it was a two-and- a-half to three hour journey, and the bus left at six on Monday mornings. Because I couldn't get into the school hostel for my first year my mother had found digs with Calum MacIver, a docker, and his wife, Annie. He was called 'Calum Cam', because he had a squint. I shared digs there with Katie Bell MacLeod from number 20 Marvig. The MacIvers were lovely people. The house was at 28 Seaforth Road, the same street where the BBC Alba studio is now.

During the first term I had measles and was staying off school to recover. It was December 16, a Saturday afternoon, and we were sitting there with a big fire on, just the three of us, Calum and Annie and myself. Suddenly there was a knock at the door and Calum was startled. It was my cousin Alex John come to tell me that my father was ill. Calum later explained that he had heard that knock several times after I had first come into the house the previous August and had got up in the night to answer an empty door.

I had to make ready. I took my wee suitcase, and Mrs McIver put in a cake and a quarter of tea and all sorts of things saying, "Och well, your Mummy will have a lot of visitors", for they well knew the situation. Then I walked out into absolutely awful, terrible snow. There was only one phone box in Marvig so I phoned the local Post Office. I had four pennies, but it was engaged. I then had to walk over a mile by myself to my Auntie Kitty Ann's. My brother Duncan had been in hospital for the previous couple of weeks with a perforated ulcer and had been at death's door, but was recovering, and so I was to travel home with him in the ambulance.

As I went along Kenneth Street the Stornoway boys were there and they started shouting, "She's a Maori, she's a Maori," and pelting me with snowballs. I'll never forget the agony of it as long as I live. All Gaelic-speaking kids from the country were called Maoris, or Mau-Maus. I suppose that's when I became conscious of my identity as a Gael.

The ambulance came to my auntie's with my brother in it and then it took us three hours to get home, he lying in one bed and I in the other. When we arrived, they were waiting at the gate and saying in Gaelic, "*Am paisde, am paisde*"; "the child, the child." I went into the house, and the whole place was in shock, it had happened so fast. So I just said, "Has anybody milked the cow?" I lit a lantern and went to the byre and got on with it – always the practical one, just like nowadays when I get bad news and I always go and make soup. I remember leaning against the cow and milking her and weeping. It was a heavy time all round, and especially for a twelve-year-old girl.

I had received a letter in the post from my father that same day but he was dead by that time I read it. It contained my school report card, which has the only signature of his that I still have. There was a letter with it, which is now lost. This was my legacy, which I find very hard to talk about, being written just before he died. He finished it by saying, "I know you're going to make it. From your ever loving Father." What a legacy!

My mother of course never wore a colour for the rest of her life, and she died in 1996. Even her petticoats were black and she had white and black crepe round her hat for two or three years. There was black dye kept at home especially for a death, when everything was dyed – all of the frocks, blouses, things like that, were dyed there, on the spot. I wore a black diamond on my coat sleeve for about two years.

I've still got about a hundred letters written to my mother at the time. Duncan kept them, and when he died his wife gave them to me. They make very interesting reading. There are some from South Georgia, from the island boys who were there at the whaling.

Shortly before my father died and while Duncan had been hovering between life and death for many days, I had a dream. In it I saw the slope down to the shore at Marvig, and I dreamt that the whole village was standing there, waiting for Duncan's wedding. As we were all waiting for the event, the boat suddenly went down in the bay. It just sank, the top of the mast disappearing under the water. In island folklore to dream of a wedding means a coming death, and my father's passing explained its prophetic nature. The boat was a symbol of the upkeep of the family. So that was the first of my precognitions.

Life went on after that, and my brothers continued to fish. They were drift net fishermen, at sea all week, and their wives did the croft work. They all married local women. I spent more time at home with my brothers than my sisters ever did, because they went away when old enough. Christy Ann went first of all to Stornoway, to the Pringles, then into service in Glasgow, working for a Jewish family. Jessie went to the Nicolson Institute and then to 'Dough School', the Domestic Science College in Glasgow, where one of her classmates was Kay Matheson, of Stone of Destiny fame. She then became a kitchen supervisor and cook in hospitals and hotels, including eventually in Skye, where she met her husband.

When my brother Duncan got married he built a house close to the family home at Marvig, as did Murdo when he was married, so we were something of a commune really, with the grandchildren all about the same ages. There were also some other characters in the community who had an immense influence without us realising it; people like Donald Alec Mackenzie, my mother's cousin, a very strong man and a committed Communist, who painted his house and boat and everything red. There was Aonghas Lachie, who made me my cradle, and who also made me a miniature creel, so that I could carry the peats on my wee back. He got a big piece of turf and shaped the willow into it then knitted more willow round it. So I had my own little creel, with a rope that I put round my shoulders and carried little bits of peat on my back along with the adults.

Aonghas Lachie lived with his sister Seonag – they were bachelor brother and spinster sister, which was quite common in the islands at one time. She was a delightful busybody and knew everything. A boat, the *Lady Marjory*, belonged to their family and Seonag used to find out how many crans of herring each boat in the village had so she knew what they were all earning per week better than their salesmen did.

Our house was quite a distance from the shore, and there was a rock halfway between the water and the house where everyone took a rest – because all household goods came by boat. One day in the late 1940s my father was carrying a big cardboard box, and sat as always on the rock to have a pipe, when Seonag came out of her door. She always had to find out what everything was, and she shouted in Gaelic, "What have you got in that box on your back Angus," and my father said *"Tigh cac"*, which means a shithouse, and she went in and closed the door and he chuckled away. She was so nosy that when she heard there was something being built she had to see it for herself. And of course, it was an Elsen dry lavatory. My father loved to tease her, and she loved to be teased. I can still see her sitting on the wee bench in the kitchen, waiting on one of the vans, Lipton's or the Co-op, or whatever van was due that day.

Another amazing person was my Auntie Christina, who lived at Halfway House, Calbost. She was very spiritual, and her spirituality and her natural psychology were amazing. She always sensed atmosphere and I remember one night she had been visiting somewhere where she had not felt at all happy, and she said, "Oh yes, he was there; he was there right enough, in his overcoat and wellingtons." She was referring to the Devil, to the presence of evil, and that he meant serious business. She was an amazing woman and I was awfully, awfully fond of her.

She was also very practical. When one of her grandsons was born, her daughter had measles and the child was born prematurely, covered in spots and apparently lifeless. The doctor concentrated on saving the mother while Auntie Christina picked up the supposedly lifeless child, wrapped him in a towel and took a mouthful of whisky. Warming it in her mouth, she opened his wee mouth and spat the whisky down his throat. H breathed, coughed and is now a strapping man – no incubator, just her presence of mind.

The Post Office was run by Angus MacFarlane, who was known as Samson. He was about the same age as my father but was late in marrying – in his forties or fifties – and I remember when he was courting. He used to run the Post Office with a rod of iron. At one time the Post office had other things apart from stamps, but that was before my time.

There were one or two in the village we were frightened of. People mentioned shell shock, but we didn't understand what that meant then. There was one man who used to go up on a hill regularly in the summer time, and swear and shout obscenities across the village, and now, as an adult, I realise that might have been Tourette's syndrome. But people just ignored it. He was never sent away or anything like that. He used to curse and swear at the top of his voice, but you got used to it and people just said, "Oh, there he goes again".

Ishbel MacLeod used to clean the school – she was known as *'Ishbel Dhomhaill'.* The Home Guard kept their helmets and things in the building, and they used to have nets over their helmets for camouflage, and she used to take the nets and wear them on her hair. And she used to steal tobacco and chew it. She kept goats and she lived in a very poor house and it was said that she was a hermaphrodite, although we didn't know what that was. We had rude rhymes about her that were passed on by the older children in school, but we hadn't a clue what it meant at all. It was just a rumour and I don't suppose anybody could ever prove it.

Later on there was Hector. Hector had been a prisoner of war, one of only a small number picked up after the *Rawalpindi*, a passenger vessel converted to an armed merchant cruiser, went down while battling better armed German battleships, early in the Second World War. Its captain, who was lost, was the father of broadcaster Ludovic Kennedy. In the seventies I took Hector to meet Ludovic and his wife Moira Shearer, the famous ballet dancer and actress, as he had been on the bridge when Kennedy's father was shot to pieces. Hector rarely spoke to anyone about his wartime experiences, but he and Kennedy spent a couple of hours together, talking in private, and later all he could say was, "Imagine a man like me meeting Moira Shearer." Hector was wonderful; and when he came home from the war he started weaving cloth and weaving stories at the same time. I've got several letters from him and they're hilarious. For a man who hadn't been educated past the local school, he had the brain of a real *avant-garde* writer. He was priceless.

I can still see how all the old men used to congregate every morning at the sea end of the village where there was a big barometer just outside the school and put the world to rights. They used to stand there looking at the barometer and smoking their pipes. It was so reminiscent of those photographs and reports of the St Kilda village parliament.

Chapter 2

Bursting with Living Timelessness

FROM five years old until I was twelve, I was at the local school at Planasker. Although the wider area had parish schools and others run by the Gaelic School Society or established by the proprietor of the island, the first formal school, Planasker School, opened in 1880 to serve Marvig and Calbost. However, its roll had contracted considerably by the time I attended.

We were really very lucky there because there was a Gaelic-speaking teacher, so we spoke both Gaelic and English in class. I have no memory of learning English although I was very proud of my first book, 'The Cat sat on the Mat'. My brothers teased me stupid and I don't know how I survived that at all. For instance, they taught me the English for *sgian*. I was very proud of that and put my hand up in class to show I knew it and the teacher said "Oh very good, what is it?" to which I said, "kniffey", because I had believed them. However, from going to school at five, with no knowledge of English, by ten when we moved to the schoolmaster's room, we were reading 'Marmion' and 'The Lady of the Lake'.

We learned other skills too. The boys had a patch of vegetables, the girls had sewing. We had to clean the lavatories every Friday;

the boys did the Boys' and the girls did the Girls', with buckets of water and brushes.

There was one girl around the village called Murdina or Murdag. She was Down's Syndrome and much older than us but we all knew her and played with her. She didn't go to school at all, but she sat on the chassis of an old lorry, and we called it Murdag's lorry. She would sit there all day. Also when we came to school there was somebody there who was an epileptic and took fits and we were shown how to take the key out of the porch door and put it on his tongue, so he wouldn't swallow his tongue. You just took it for granted. It was the same with my father being a diabetic; you thought everybody had it. So when I subsequently came to work with disabled people it never bothered me one bit and it still doesn't. No matter how disabled a person is, it doesn't put me up or down and I think the grounding came from primary school.

Our play was often making *bothags* – we'd gather bits of broken china and tins and things like that and make little houses in nooks in the rocks. We didn't have hidey holes or anything like that; these were nooks, little shelves and one would be the bedroom and one would be the kitchen and so on, and you'd gather all sorts of bits and pieces like bits of rusting iron. You might make a fender from a bit of wheel from a cart or something like that. And at school, play was mostly games, and they were in English, although we didn't really speak English, and I don't understand how these games got to the village school. There were songs in English; *The Farmer's in His Den*, and we had the obvious, *Ring-a-Ring-a-Roses* and we had versions of *London Bridge* and all that sort of stuff. We had skipping games such as *We All Fall Out* and ball games like *One, Two, Three A-leerie*, although we didn't sing, "I saw Kate McLeary" or "Mrs Cleary" which I didn't hear until

I came to Edinburgh. There were no equivalents in Gaelic apart from a few very rude ones that I can't mention!

It was in the schoolhouse that my parents got married, because there was no church and the meeting-house wasn't built then I don't think. Everything happened in the school – social evenings, concerts and things. I didn't know about it but another girl from the village, who was older than me, told me that my father used to run concerts and encourage them all to do little plays and things. I wrote a poem about when it was closed in 1973:

> Planasker school was closed this year
> Planasker where my father married my mother,
> Planasker where I felt my first smell of coal,
> And where the cocoa was strong on winter days
> Planasker where I learnt to high jump
> Planasker where I learned that there were things to be
>   learned.
> Coming home by Creagan Alick
> With Aonghas Thormoid shouting that he would
> "Scythe our legs for treading on the uncut grass"
> Coming home, stopping at Ishbel Fhionnlaigh's
> To hear the drips of rain coming through the roof
> And making music in the assorted receptacles.
> Stopping at Christy a' Cheannaic's for
> A potato out of the *prais* and a word of comfort.
> Coming home, to my father
> Mending endless herring nets.
> Running to Planasker on a spring morning
> Running to Planasker after a summer's dinner time
> Leaping the *claisen*, bursting with living timelessness.
> Leaving Planasker for Education
> Leaving Planasker full of anticipation

And coming back –
To Planasker.
To dirty windows, to grassy playgrounds
To mossy steps – to a closed porch.
Planasker school was closed this year.

☙

Around the first of May was always a very important time in our lives as everything was got ready for the summer fishing season. Before the use of synthetic materials the nets were treated to preserve them by '*cairteadh*' or 'barking the nets'. This was done at home in an enormous cauldron of boiling water with *cutch*, an extract of bark of some sort, added to make a very strong, dark brown solution. Afterwards the nets were hung on poles to dry.

Throughout the winter months whole herring nets were strung from corner to corner across the window ready for mending. You would clip off the loose mesh with a knife, which would then be held under an arm, and you would take a miniature shuttle or *snathaid-charaidh* and start. These were made of bone. You could get ivory ones but it was a ploy to make one out of spalebone or horn. When there were no holes left in that section it came down and the next part was done. You worked the whole net, and it was a huge one, until it was finished. And there was a mess; there were clippings all over the floor. We always took the net down on a Saturday night so that it was not up on the Sabbath.

This was done mainly by my father after he had stopped going to sea, but I was mending nets too before I started going to school. You were just taught how to do it. Often, and especially during the war, men like Aonghas Lachie, funny old Shonnie Dhomhnuill Bhain and others, would come to help because we had a wireless.

It was in my mother and father's room, a huge mahogany box on the table. My father would go out and switch it on and when it came to the nine o'clock news someone would say, "There's the gongs", and they would all troop out to the good room to listen to it. My mother would make tea and scones with crowdie and things for them coming back out and then they would discuss and put the world to rights, after hearing the news. And of course the accumulator battery would invariably fail. You may have heard about the woman from Cromore who asked was there anything on the news today and when they told her that unfortunately the accumulator had gone down she said, "Oh Dear! Was there any locals on it?"

The net buoys were made of hide of some kind and had wooden tops with a bung in them and they were painted in quarters, white and blue. They didn't always all need to be blown up but some of them needed a little extra air. I don't know what kind of leather or skin they were made from, but they were strong and difficult to inflate. They were blown up by mouth, so everybody ended up with tar round their lips that you had to take off with margarine.

Then we readied the litters for the boy's bunks on the boat. My mother and I would make them by sowing flour sacks together. The sacks were washed, opened out and bleached by laying them on the grass in the sun. Then they were filled with dry straw, absolutely stuffed in. We had these in our own beds too, our box beds were filled with straw with the mattress placed on top.

When they were ready we carried all these things down to the shore. Then it all went into the small rowing boat and was taken out to the fishing boat. I can see it and smell it all yet, with the forget-me-nots and primroses and bluebells all the way down to the water. The rowing boat made several trips and before long you could see the stove was going by the smoke coming out. The kids used to sit on a hill, half way between the house and the shore, watching to see which boat would go out first. The boats had wonderful names; there was the *Maggie MacDonald*, the *Trust*, the *Lady Marjory*. We had the *Triumph* and then the *Ebenezer*, which had been called the *Fancy* when they first brought it from Badachro, Gairloch. She was painted blue and she was lovely, but then of course my brothers started being called "the fancy boys". We could not have huge, blond, rugged men being called that in the 1940s so my father changed it to the *Ebenezer*, after 1 Samuel 7:12:

> Then Samuel took a stone, and set it between Mizpeh and Shen, and called the name of it Ebenezer, saying, Hitherto hath the LORD helped us.

℞

I loved to see all the boats going out on a beautiful May Day, then they would come home on the Saturday, with all sorts of things from Stornoway; *The People's Journal*, *The Weekly News*, loaves from J & E's, sheeps' heads from Noonie's, dry goods from *Buth Thearlaich* and things like that.

It was in the Minch they were fishing and only for herring. Latterly, in the sixties, they got a special winch for prawn fishing, because the herring stock was going down, but they sold it after a year because they were killing so much fish. They were true conservationists before the word came into common usage. They were drift netters and so they got the best herring. They never got spent herring, just the very big ones and they did not kill anything unnecessarily. And they did the great lines too, with baited hooks for eels, lithe, skate, cod; big, big white fish that were salted and dried. Small cuddies, or *cudaigean*, were caught in large numbers just with a rod from the rocks by the shore. We prepared our own herring and mackerel in the late autumn. We laid a big barrel of herring and a big barrel of mackerel in salt and it made its own pickle and that was our staple diet, although we always had meat on Sundays and when we had visitors. The dried fish used to hang from rafters in the old shop.

The way they shared out the catch was fascinating. The skipper, Duncan, would put the fish down and then he or somebody else would stand with their back turned to them and throw a stone over their shoulder saying, "That's for so-and-so" and, "That's for so-and-so". That way there was no arguments or preference. It was casting lots, *cruinn*, just your luck and done without dispute. Then when they got home of course, we'd start gutting and I'd have to go to all the widows of people who didn't have fishermen in the family with their share. *Daithead* we called it, which obviously comes from 'diet'. Everything was shared. My brother Murdo still does that. He's now well into his 80s and he sets a net most nights; he's down there at six o'clock in the morning and when he gets a good catch, he cuts and fillets them down at the shore, then leaves them at all the houses he passes by. He's amazing. When he got his pacemaker he bought a new engine for the boat on his way home from hospital in Inverness.

When the ring-netters started working in pairs, everything changed. They used to come right round from the East Coast, and that caused an awful stushie. My father once shot across their bows. When the Minch was closed I was moved to write this to the *Stornoway Gazette* and I can hardly read it still for the pain of it:

Sir, I was prompted to write by the latest development in our fishing history. I refer to the sale recently of the *Seafarer*, the last Lewis drifter to fish out of Stornoway. Whether we like it or not, the blame must rest on the vandals who destroyed the seabed with any thought of conservation or the future of the industry. The old story of the fast buck, subsidised by large government grants, to enable the implements of destruction to become more sophisticated. *Sgadan balaich Mharabhig* – "Marvig boys' herring" – was known throughout the island. Would anyone call herring the mush that gets vacuumed out of the holds of purse netters. My anger is made greater by the unbearable sadness of knowing the beautiful bay that once anchored the *True Love*, the *Maggie MacDonald*, the *Trust*, the *Lady Marjory* and many more now lies empty, and that the village children won't know the joy that we felt at watching the boats leave on Monday evenings and coming back on Saturdays, laden with fish for neighbours and goodies for the children. I remember as a child being taken to the back of Drumanais by my father to see the first pair of ring-netters at work, and his saying that this was the beginning of the end, and how right he was. If the old people were alive to see the new fishing methods at work they would be horrified. The irony is that it is called progress. Shame on our governments to let the situation get out of hand. Salutations to balaich Mharabhig for having supplied the community for so long. As for the *Seafarer*. If you see her at Ullapool pier, give her a wave, and I'll carry on in my imagination, picking forget-me-nots for the fishermen on Mondays.

෪

We used to go out to the shore and get cockles, with spades. And at spring tides we used to go out to Tòraidh, a sea island, where they put sheep to graze sometimes. It's quite a bit out, and has really white coral, and we used to fill sacks with shellfish; razor fish and big clams and the like, for there were wonderful feeds just there for the taking. As for scallops, you could see them open and they used to tickle them with a bamboo rod, and they'd snap on it and they'd bring them into the boat. And you only got the big ones – again, conservation. And we never ever ate shellfish if there wasn't an 'R' in the month. You stopped in April and you didn't start again until September. I still go by that, because they need that time to regenerate.

I used to have to deliver a fish to every house on Saturdays. You put your fingers up the gills and out the mouth of the fish and carried them to those who didn't have people at sea. And if anybody's cow was dry you always took milk to them. Sharing is still with me, very, very much so. My mother wouldn't have anybody leave the house without giving them something; a quarter of tea or an orange or whatever. Sharing was part of life.

We always had a boll of flour and a boll of oatmeal. The oatmeal came in hessian bags and it was horrible when you got to the bottom of it and you got hessian hairs in your porridge. The bags had the names of the mills on them, for instance Herdman's Mills, grain merchants in Leith. And the flour bags were then used for all sorts of things; for clootie dumplings and everything. They were of such good quality heavy linen, more like really thick cotton or calico.

We never made yeast bread at all but we used yeast for making beastie beer. We used a huge glass vessel that must have come from when my father had the shop. It was about two foot tall with a round glass bowl on top of it. I don't know what happened to it. It had what looked like slugs or maggots at the bottom but that was the yeast, which multiplied. You got a bit of the yeast culture from someone else and you would take it from there.

At the peat cutting, they took the beer and whey out in pails to the moor for their thirst.

Every Saturday, my mother would make big scones; huge bannocks cut in four, and she would make anything up to forty or fifty of them. Then oatcakes were made over an open fire in the kitchen scullery. She used to put the oatcakes on the griddle for a wee while then stand them up on the hearth to dry out. Clootie dumpling was made every Saturday. The baking went on all day long.

Then there was making crowdie. The thick milk was put in the dresser, a wooden cupboard, and the cream was taken off and made into butter. We used to make the butter when there was enough cream, but it wasn't a regular thing. There were no fridges or anything and, of course it wasn't pasteurised, so it was natural yoghurt really, that set by itself. We put that on a pan at the side of the stove and gradually it formed crowdie with whey beneath. Then you took the crowdie and squeezed it, to get all of the whey out, which was wonderful to drink; bitter, bitter green whey. That was used to make the scones as well, as was buttermilk. Everything was used and everything was recycled. The dogs and the cattle got all the leftovers.

Saturday was also a very busy day as you also prepared the Sunday meal then. The soup was made on Saturday night. The boys – my brothers – usually brought over a sheep's head at the weekend, and it was great. You put the tongs in the fire until they were red hot and then singed it before putting it in a pail of water with slices of bread to take the taste of the singe away. The soup it made was great, with lots of barley and turnips and things. Because there was not much space, just the one stove and so many of us to feed, the meat was usually cooked in the soup, and then sliced. Latterly of course there were roasts and all sorts of things, but I'm going right back to my childhood when we were all together in the house. Your soup was what the meat had been boiled in, and you had the boiled meat afterwards. I still do that. Since I'm on my own, it's much easier to do a one-pan meal. It wasn't cooked on the Saturday, but everything was prepared then, and so it was simmering on the stove on Sunday morning. At communion time I would go my Aunty Peggy's if she was in church to make sure her soup was all right, because a lot of visitors came on communion weekends, something that still happens. At Murdo's house last year they had over thirty for lunch; it's like a folk festival. Everybody gathered in the one house where the sessions are going on; or the biblical dispute and discussion and psalm-singing. The pudding too was made on a Saturday night; trifle usually, or jellies, but nothing was done on Sunday; we didn't even wash the dishes until Monday.

We would have our dinner when the adults came from church. On Sunday my brothers always got their breakfasts in bed. My mother and I made trays up, with bacon and egg and fried dumpling and sausages, because they'd been at sea all week and we'd put them into their rooms. They slept together, two in that room and two in the other. They would then get up and my mother would milk the cow and go off to church, a five mile walk to Gravir. The boys took bicycles and left later, but the women and older men, they walked there and back every Sunday. I was too young to walk that distance and stayed home with my father who could not go because of his diabetes. When they got home, we had our dinner before Sunday school in the village meeting house, and church again in the evening. Winter, I remember, was the only time we sat down together, really, because there was work all the time. However, it wasn't rushing like we are nowadays as everybody had time to stop and smell the roses. On Sunday afternoons my father would read to us from 'The Pilgrim's Progress' or 'The Golden Treasury' or something like that and I would sit with my head on my mother's knee and she would look for nits, because they were quite common, particularly with so many kids living in blackhouses. I still bribe my granddaughters to look in my hair. I suppose it's because of this memory of complete security.

Another job on a Saturday was plucking something. On special occasions there would be chicken from our own hens. My mother used to go into the hen house and put a finger up the bums of each of the hens and if there was an egg there it got reprieved. Practicality again: why kill a hen if it's about to lay? And she would just go and wring them herself, then cut their beaks and hang them by their legs in the corner of the scullery until they were bled. And then we'd pluck them.

I used to go to Donald Alex, the communist, for *cock's eggs*. My mother sent me because we didn't have a cockerel, which he had, but we had a broody hen, so I would take a dozen eggs in to him and he would give me a dozen eggs in return, which went under our hen. It was a sort of barter.

We ate a lot of cormorants as well. Oh, I loved cormorant. It's very dark meat, slightly fishy, but it has a wonderful taste of its own. The soup we made with it I now make with pheasant, and everybody asks me what it is but I don't tell them. It's just onion and thick oatmeal. You use the cormorant stock or *sùgh* and chopped onion and handfuls of oatmeal, but in my guesthouse I used to put thyme and sage in it too. Well you can't get cormorant now so it's made with the pheasant carcasses, because I'd serve pheasant a lot in season and always made the soup from their bones. I put a spoonful of sherry in the plates before dishing it up.

You couldn't put the sherry into the soup because it would make it sour, but if you put it in the plates and pour it over it's a great success. So that's where I got that from, from eating cormorants.

We did not eat guga, as gannet chicks are called locally. That was done in Ness, it was concentrated in that area. And again, it's a family thing; you would have to be invited. It's reminiscent, somehow, of life on St Kilda. It's a fraternal thing, to be invited to go on the hunt. We used to eat a heron occasionally, and blackcock, grouse, snipe and masses of trout. It was all local, just taken on the common grazing, but they used to do dreadful things like kill otters as well. There was a man in the village had a special dog for killing otters in order to get the skin, which he dried and posted to somebody who made fur coats. They used to do the same with rabbits; the shed wall was always full of rabbit skins, nailed up to dry out and when there was a dozen they were parcelled up to be sent off to England and money would come in return.

Planting the potatoes was a dreadful time, because it was always cold, bitterly cold, and you put the manure on with your hands. There was a big pile of it outside the byre. This was March and April. It was always freezing, there were no rubber gloves or anything and it was all done by spade, as the lazy beds were so narrow because of the rocky terrain. It was always the young ones who got the job of putting in the potatoes – and who was the youngest? Myself of course. The men dug a trench and we put them in. The manure had already been put out in creels, and you put it on top before they would come over and you'd change places and do the other side. It took two or three weeks, because we planted everywhere. When all the land was tilled it went right down to the shore. And especially I remember autumn evenings when we were raking the grass, and all the other croft families would be out raking too. But it's all barren now.

It was year about crop rotation. If there were potatoes one year it was corn and oats the next and so on. The corn was made into a high stack and was used as required for fodder and for the litter for the beds. When it came to the following summer the stacks were demolished, the sheaves bashed on the rocks and the seeds gathered into a tarpaulin. We didn't have a mill. The seeds were used for hen feed and for sowing the following spring. The great fun was that it was full of mice, and dogs would have a whale of a time chasing them and the occasional rat from under the stooks where they'd hidden all winter.

We had a vegetable garden, although it was not all that common. People planted turnips and carrots I suppose, but we had all sorts of things like leeks and lettuce and blackcurrant bushes, and we grew lupins. We had a lovely garden. It was probably my father's idea. Having been 'away', he brought all these things back. We were accused of eating grass because we ate lettuce. We used to dip the lettuce in sugar. There were blaeberries out on the moor, oh, gosh, lots. We took tiny, tiny little black ones we called *corrach-a-mhiag*. There was a wee island just by where we had the peats and there were stepping stones out to it and it was covered in blaeberries. But it also had *bratag-fhraoich*, very long creepy-crawlies with yellow and black fur on them, furry caterpillars. They were huge. There was heather and honeysuckle as well on this wee island.

We ate really, really well. We didn't realise it, of course. Our own milk, our own butter, our own sheep, mutton, fish; everything was there. We sent parcels away to Glasgow during the war, eggs especially, corrugated cardboard boxes with a dozen holes in them and 'Eggs with care' written on them. You wrapped them in newspaper, and sometimes maybe only half of them would arrive whole. Then you'd get the box back with apples or something in them.

Our water was wonderful. We had the best well because it never got any sun. It was always full and when other wells in the village dried, ours always had water in it. We stopped using it when water came on tap. I cleaned it one summer when I was back home and they all called me a fool. Oh, the water, it was just amazing. I suppose it's now full of bracken. I have a poem about that well:

I climbed over barbed wire to get to you,
I broke through several spiders' webs,
In one upward step, I spanned the rock
I used to have to slide down,
There was no path left, or right
But I went straight to you.

I could not see you for growth,
I tore away the ferns and bailed you
Until you were almost empty,
I scrubbed you and dried you out,
Four hours, they said, and you would be full again.

The mist was heavy over all,
Blocking out the past, the present and almost the future
An unattached bleat was the only sound.

At four o'clock the mist had risen, partly
Part of the past was present
But there was a slight scum on your surface
So I bailed you out again.

At eight I could see the grey coast,
New houses growing up, a boat or two,
The fallow lazy beds.

The mist was almost gone then,
And you were almost pure.

I took two pails of your clean water home.
They said I was a fool.

☙

There were grocery vans. They used to come from Stornoway once a week, and I remember they always called over to us for a cup of tea, because it was thirty-two miles from the town. I remember the first time I saw a banana. The van man had them 'under the counter' and he gave me one. That was just after the war.

Of course, Saturday was also the washing day. The boys came home with filthy clothes, having been at sea all week, heavy trousers or *briogais chlo Bucach*, jeans and jumpers and fishermen's sweaters, those canvas things, and that was all done in the loch. Everything was washed down at the loch. The fire was made there because it was easier. There was no water in the house, and it was easier to take the washing to the water than to take the water to the washing, and you'd go down with a shovel of embers and start a big peat fire under a big pan, and everything was boiled. Everything was boiled, and then thrashed in the water and carried home in a creel and put out to dry.

It would have to come in on a Sunday but sometimes it went on the wee fence in front of the door so nobody would see it. But it couldn't go on the line, oh no. And you still can't put your washing out yet on a Sunday. Some newcomers do, and they're frowned upon. They learn quite soon not to do it.

☙

The sheep were clipped in early summer. We used to sell fleeces after the sheep were sheared in summer time. That was a wonderful, wonderful day, the fank day. All the men left early in the morning with the dogs to gather the sheep. There was a loch where we had our peats and we would walk round the loch in the afternoon to pick up all the wool and stuff it into sacks.

Wool was once dyed naturally and when I was young there was one woman, Seonag, the last of them who still did this. I used to go and scrape rocks for the *crotal* for dyeing and she would go up to another loch above her house, *Loch-nam-Peitan*. She had a big cauldron up there and she brewed the dye from the *crotal*. The *crotal* came from the rocks themselves. It's like little grey bubbles, like a lichen or moss. You had to scrape it off, and we'd use what was once a spoon but with one side flat from the years of scraping. She would dye the wool, but it was a very, very bitter cinnamon, orangey brown colour, not a very nice colour at all, very harsh. Later on at college I learned to make dye with onions and things; onion peel makes a most beautiful, delicate, pale, creamy yellow. There were masses of things they could have used and I'm sure they did at one time, but I just came in at the very tail end of this happening in the village

My mother would send a flour bag of washed fleece to Brora, a huge big bag and I would write on it with a pen, 'T M Hunter, woollen mills, Brora'. That would go in the post and back would come knitting wool and blankets, whatever you ordered. I'm not sure whether you paid for the blankets, but I think it was an exchange thing.

Everybody sent to Brora for their knitting wool for the jerseys and socks for the fishermen. My mother knitted socks constantly. In fact she was nearly ninety-six when she died and she had a pair of socks on the go. Her hands were never ever idle. You can see photographs of women carrying creels of peats on their backs and knitting all the time as they walked. Apart from special items bought in Stornoway everything else was bought through catalogues; all clothes and such things came from flimsy brochures such as those from JD Williams and Oxendales. There is a story that during the war a woman from Point sent a box of eggs to JD Williams with the note, 'Don't tell Oxendales'. My mother would write to them in Manchester, 'Please send blah, blah, blah, blah ... and oblige. Yours faithfully ...'

It was very rare for fishermen to be involved in tweed making. You were either-or and the fishermen would never wear Harris Tweed. There was one man who had a wee blackhouse in Calbost, he did both. I don't remember him, but I remember his family. He wove, but quite loose weaving.

ᚩ

I was out at the peats every day until they were all brought home. I would walk round the loch and fill all the bags, and carry as many as I could down to the shore. Then Donald would row over and we would load the boat with ten to twenty at a time to ferry them over. We would play games with the dog who would be sitting on top of them. If you'd say "*mach!*"; "out!" the minute he heard it he leapt off the boat and swam home. And you'd say "*Co tha mach a-rathad?*" "Who's going out the road?" and he was off, swimming.

And then there was the stacking, of course. You had to carry them on your back from our side of the loch, which was large and deep, up to the house. It was absolutely non-stop, but I remember how one year we left quite a lot of cut peat there over the winter; we didn't take it all over in the autumn, because it would have taken a long time. We would stack them across there and bring them over as needed. And my brother Murdo John went and got a sheet of corrugated iron, we used to call it a plate, and he made holes in it and put a rope in it and he walked on the ice, right round the loch, not across it. Rather than carrying them back, he got three bags of peats, quite heavy, and sledged it right along the edge of the loch. So our bad winters are not all to do with climate change, it was like that in the past too.

Donald Alec Mackenzie, a first cousin of my mother's, used to bring home spiders from the heather on the moors to keep the moths down. He'd bring matchboxes full of them home and let them loose all over the house. He was the communist who painted his house red. He was a real character.

It was just non-stop and in the long summer holidays, it was just work, work, work, with cutting the grass and raking it and getting ready for the autumn, cutting and bringing the peats home, washing all the linen in the kists in the shed. The kists came out every summer and everything was put on lines to air. I can still smell them. There was a long evening dress, I don't know where it came from, but every summer we took out the kists that were full of sheets and blankets, there was this lace evening dress in dark blue. Now whether father had brought it home for mother and she didn't want it, I don't know but I used to put this dress on and put a belt round it and put a hat on and an umbrella and I used to go and visit all the houses and do a wee turn. Yes, it had started then.

I always associate that with another summer smell, that of the roof being tarred. Our house had a bitumen roof and that had to be re-coated by my father. Later on they put a slate roof on it but the smell of tar I still associate with home. The original house is no longer there because Donald and his family built a new one, and my mother moved in with them. In those days you got a grant for the new house but had to knock down the old building, in case you rented it out or something like that which was a shame.

ର

Our music was psalm singing, mostly. Morning and night at home, there would be a prayer said, a chapter read and four verses of a psalm sung in the traditional manner before we were on our knees for the last prayer. First thing in the morning and last thing at night, and I used to shout down, "Say the book so that I can go to sleep." So I went to sleep when they were singing. We didn't sing psalms in English at all, but we read the Bible in English in school, and when we were reading it there were words that we just didn't know, but we just said them as they sounded. My brother Murdo is one of the last great precentors of the Free Church.

My cousin Mary Ann had a gramophone and I remember she had records by Kitty MacLeod who sang traditional Gaelic song and by Alan MacLean. We learned Gaelic songs and English songs and in the secondary school in Stornoway we did action songs in Gaelic.

Duncan played the pipes, Murdo played the accordion, so there was some music at home, but I'm not terribly aware of singing other than the psalms. It was just something you absorbed without knowing where you heard it. However, I do know that Marvig was noted for its bards and piping.

My father used to put on concerts in the school and he would to go to dances in Stornoway, but my mother wouldn't go, so he took the local teacher as his partner. Mother just didn't seem to have the time for music, "Nonsense, all that nonsense."

There was dancing on the road at the crossroads and at the wee bridge to Dhomhnaill na Banntraich's. I don't remember this, but my brother Donald tells the story beautifully of how there was a holy man living close to this bridge where they used to play accordions and melodeons and have dancing. The man went to see Roddy MacKinnon to tell him his sons were sinners for playing the accordion and as he lectures him MacKinnon says, "Well, I was just thinking I was going to get them a bigger one!" It was in that very house that the last member of that family died last year, and an Englishman has bought it. I used to go and visit the old *cailleach* there. She had five sons in the Second World War and she lost three of them. Donald said to me, "I remember dancing on that floor," and I said, "What do you mean?" And he explained how it was the last house in the village that had an earth floor. It was of corrugated iron on the outside; two solid gable ends, corrugated iron sides and roof, and with an earth floor. They sent for all the young people between the villages to dance on it all night, to pack it down.

ଔ

My mother rarely travelled and we never went on holidays as such. During the summer, she and I would go to her relatives in Balallan, which was a couple of hours by bus in those days. It's a long village, the longest on the island, where the road from South Lochs and Harris meet. We have cousins there and we used to go and see them once a year. Then we would go to Cromore and Gravir to visit, but only for a day. We would walk the five miles over the moors where there was a track because it's much longer by road. Those were our outings. My mother would only go to Stornoway once a year but she would start feeling sick when she heard the sound of the bus, so we used to pick bunches of bog myrtle and she would carry them with her on the bus so she wouldn't smell the petrol. That was her outing and she would maybe buy a hat or a frock.

Then there was Halloween. You always knew when Halloween was near because somebody would send a parcel of apples from Stornoway. They were hidden away until the night but you could still smell them in the house. We always had Halloween on the 12th November, because we still kept the Julian calendar. It was quite a thing for the children. They made us masks out of cardboard and we dressed up and went round the houses. We didn't get anything. It wasn't like going round today with a sack to see how much money you could make. That didn't come into it. You just went to amuse people and for them to guess who you were; and of course they would never guess. We just went to my Aunty Kate's and to my Auntie Peggy's and I think that was it, and they used to do a big thick oatmeal bannock with threepenny or sixpenny bits in it, about half an inch thick and you had to find your token. It was all about dressing up. We didn't call it guising, we didn't know that word, but it was quite important to us. We dooked for apples; there were no treacle scones or anything like that. It was apples and fancy dress and home-made masks.

We had our superstitions such as the fear of walking out and seeing *tiene biorach* or will o' the wisp. Also, there were all sorts of premonitions of death; dogs howling at night, that kind of thing and other superstitions too. I remember when the *Mamie* fishing boat went down in January 1962. They were on their way back from Stornoway to Marvig and she went on the rocks after the engine failed. My brothers wanted to go and help them, but the coastguard wouldn't let them, and one of those on board, James Mackenzie, was drowned. They threw out a lifeline to James to swim to shore but he was lost. My brothers were furious because they knew the underwater channels better than anyone. The others, Kenny and his younger sister, Kirsty-Ann were rescued after over seven hours in horrendous conditions. Apparently years before, some people, such as those who babysat for James and his wife, would hear noises – a terrible banging at the window. When they brought James' coffin it wouldn't go in the door because of the narrow passageway and they had to take out the window. I was aware of superstitions from an early age, especially those to do with death and ghosts and premonitions. These were taken seriously and still are to this day.

Death and funerals were treated with great, great dignity. When there was a death in the village, or in any of the neighbouring communities of Marvig, Calbost, and Cromore, or even Gravir sometimes, all the boats would come ashore and they would not go out again until the day after the funeral. Because there were fishermen from the different villages in each boat there was a hush everywhere and it would last for three days. The people of the village where the death was did not put their washing out and we children were not allowed to play outside or anything like that. That doesn't happen at all now, even there.

The funeral service was always held in the house, the people sitting all night with the coffin. I believe that started first in the old blackhouses where people lived with their animals at the lower end and it would take time for the coffin to be made and delivered. There were bible readings, psalm-singings and prayers all evening while the corpse was in the house. Most people would go away after the prayers, but the young men of the village sat there all night sharing stories and jokes. A wake was a social occasion, and I remember my brother Donald saying how he was surprised a judgement didn't come on them for the carry on they had. Funerals would be a male-only affair at the graveyard, but in the last few years the women have started going too as I saw when my sister died recently. There were so many men carrying the coffin. They were in twos, and walked so many paces before another pair would take over and so on. MacDiarmid describes it beautifully in his poem 'An Island Funeral'.

There was no drink involved at all, unlike in the Southern Isles and Ireland where it's normal. That was never ever the case at home. The men might take a dram to warm themselves up when they came back after the burial, but drink and death were not compatible.

As a rule, drinking was not a significant part of village life although everybody had a bottle of brandy for medicinal purposes and the men might have a shared keg on special nights. One of the few times there was drinking was New Year, when there would be a glass of port or sherry for the women, but they were just to taste it and pass it on to the next person. However, there was nothing at Christmas. Also, when the merchant seamen came home they always had half bottles and they would go round the old men in the village and give them a dram, and bring them cigarettes and tobacco 'from away'. If they came home on the bus about ten o'clock at night or later even, they would always come to our house first so that their mothers wouldn't smell drink off them. Our mother would give them a cup of tea and a scone.

∞

I remember my brother Duncan going off to the war with his number on his sailor's bonnet, LTK X529787. Once when he was home on leave, he brought me a locket with 'Rio' on it, with palm trees, a sort of translucent thing. I don't know what happened to it.

Duncan came off the ferry one evening and was home for only a few days. His bus back to Stornoway left on Wednesday afternoon.

It normally went in the morning at about ten o'clock but on Wednesdays all the shops in Stornoway were shut in the afternoon so it came later for the passengers going on the boat, which left at midnight, and you had to spend the whole evening somewhere in Stornoway. Usually the men went to the Sailor's Home, and there was a waiting room in the town hall, and everybody had relatives there anyway. I didn't want to say goodbye to Duncan and so I went to hide. We had so many sheds round our house and I hid in one which had the flywheel of an engine stored there. This was very large, heavy and difficult to move. However, when the bus came, the flywheel fell on my legs. There I was hiding in the shed with the flywheel over my legs and I couldn't move, so I was stuck. Duncan came looking for me as he wouldn't go on the bus without seeing me, and eventually he found me pinned to the floor by the huge thing. It's so clear in my mind. The flywheel hurt my shinbones – they were black. I was so skinny anyway with legs like knitting needles, but nothing was broken. But it just kind of toppled on me and I would have been there for hours if Duncan hadn't come to look for me to say goodbye. That must have been near the end of the war. He was in Australia and Hong Kong and places like that in the Royal Navy. That was the trouble then, you didn't know if they were coming back, because there were still ships being blown up. He was seventeen when I was born so he would have been in his twenties then.

Donald did his National Service in the Royal Navy as a stoker but Murdo John had a dispensation because he was a fisherman. He went down to somewhere in England first, then to Rosyth on the Forth, so he was away for a couple of weeks each year until National Service was over.

Chapter 3

A Teenager in Stornoway

I WENT to Stornoway for the first time in the post van. We were on our way to visit my Uncle Alec Murdo's wife's people at Breasclete on the west side of Lewis, but I thought I was going to Glasgow, because Alec lived in Glasgow but his wife came from Breasclete. I wrote about my first impressions of the town sometime in the 1960s:

> What does a street look like ... the Royal Mail is very sacred, it brings good news and bad and parcels smelling of apples at Halloween, and we are bundled into the back of it. Every car that comes towards us we have to lie flat among the lumpy sacks of good and bad news. Suddenly trees. Did anyone ever see so many trees? They cut the sun away from the road. I have never seen any, apart from the few rowans growing out from the rock crevices in the village, and the heavy July honeysuckle dripping in the sea below the *croit*. Trees that brush the sides of the mail on its way to the promised land, Stornoway. Keith Street. A toilet with a chain ... oh, how many unnecessary trips just to pull that chain. Johnny the milkman with his *claudach* capable hand, turning the tap at your request for a quart please, not knowing what a quart was. Are

you from the country, blone? The bakery in Scotland Street. A blonde girl with a shiny new bike. JS's with its special smell and its sacks of victuals. Seagulls that sounded different from the ones at home. The masts swinging basket after basket of herring onto the quay and a little lady shuffling along Point Street in her slippers. A few years later, bubblegums for a penny in Capaldi's, half a crown thrown from my brother's boat on to the pier, only to roll into the shimmering water …

Later, I used to go over for a week to my Auntie Kitty Ann's and stay there, but by the age of twelve I was in my first year at the Nicolson Institute. I had wonderful high school years. I was in digs with the MacIvers for the first year in Stornoway and there was another girl from the village, Katy Bell, in the same house, and we shared a bed. This was quite usual back in 1950 and nobody thought anything of it. Across from the bedroom window there was a travelling fair and lying in bed at night I heard them play *The Tennessee Waltz*, and *Your Cheatin' Heart*, and I thought to myself, "I've made it, I'm in the big city."

After my father's death during that first term I felt so alone in Stornoway. However, as a child I did not have to dress in black like my mother and the other women in the family. But I still had to wear the black patch, a black diamond on my coat, for two years to mark me out as one who had lost a parent. I only had the one coat and the following year, when it was social time, with Christmas dances at the school, I used to snip it off and sew it back on again when I went home, and that in itself brought great guilt. I still remember doing that, and feeling the guilt of it, but you couldn't go to a social with your frock on and a black patch on your coat. And of course I had to leave the choir, because my father was dead and singing just wasn't on. I left and never went back. It was absolutely hellish.

39

After a year I got a place in the Louise Carnegie Girls' Hostel which was converted from the Imperial Hotel in the early 1920s. Nowadays An Lanntair, the arts centre, occupies the site. After the old hostel was knocked down there was a car park for years and years, and when it was redeveloped there was a lot of controversy about the height of the new building. But it's very pleasing and the restaurant upstairs is in the corner is where my room, Room 10 was, and if I'm there I sit and think, "I slept here for five years."

The hostel accommodated girls from Uig, Lochs, Carloway, Ness, Shawbost and Bragar. While some got home at weekends, the South Lochs and Uig girls only got home once a term. There were fifty-two of us, and the regime was tremendously strict. We were in every night at half-past seven and studied, under supervision, from then until nine. Then we had an hour for recreation before bedtime with lights out at 10.30. We were up at seven, breakfasted at eight, and we shared bathrooms of course. One didn't shower every morning then. In fact I don't think there were showers, but baths, for which there was a rota.

That's where many friendships began that still endure. One of the closest friends I made at the hostel was Mary Morrison from Lakefield, Bragar. She is now Lady Mary MacAulay. We see each other quite often. Then there was my friend Christine Fletcher, who died not so long ago in Skye. I knew her very well as she was the matron's daughter. We held a fifty year class reunion in 2010 and it was amazing to see so faces from the past; such as Donald, a minister in Carloway who stayed with me for the Assembly some years ago and whom I still call 'Fish' and another lad who left school at fifteen and was a sea captain by the time he was twenty-five.

We had porridge every morning of course, but at lunchtime we used to come down from the school to the hostel. It varied but you always knew what was coming. It was pie and beans on Thursdays and so on. It was a fixed menu with very few treats but the food was good and it was properly cooked as we always had a good cook. After lunch, if I ran, I could go down to the pier and see my brothers. They left home in Marvig on Mondays and came home on Saturdays, but they were in Stornoway every day to land their catch, and they'd throw up a shilling or two to me sometimes.

Then we would go to Woolies and get tuppence worth of broken biscuits. They had big boxes of biscuits with glass lids on them, but they had one with broken ones, and people used to buy them and eat them on the way up to school.

At the weekends, when there were so few of us there, we used to sneak down and go into the fridge to have midnight feasts. I can still hear that fridge humming in the middle of the night. We would sneak bits and pieces away, tins of fruit and things like that, and gather in a room, giggling. We thought nobody knew, but apparently they did and they just let us get on with it. There were two staircases, with one, the 'Dame's stair', just for the matron and the teachers which we were not allowed to use. We had to go round to the back stair, and it was a kind of dare for us to go up the main one. As the matron's daughter my closest friend Christine could use it as her mother had the sitting room and bedroom upstairs.

There was always somebody in charge of each room and eventually I became head girl of Room 10, which was the largest, with seven beds. It looked on to the cinema and the pier, so we used to watch from the window to see who was coming out of the pictures and if there were teachers there. You know there was nothing secret as to who was romancing and who was seeing whom. And then we used to watch the boat leaving. It left at half-past midnight and we would always wonder who would be the first of us to go off on it, to see the mainland.

On Sundays we had to go to church both morning and evening and we could walk in the castle grounds in the afternoon. Everybody in Stornoway walked through the castle grounds on a Sunday afternoon, around by the River Creed, where you met all sorts of people. That took up the afternoon before we had to go to church again at night. We always had sweeties in church, which were passed along in a bag. You didn't look at them, you just took one and popped it in your mouth. Well, I remember once somebody passing them along, but it was cold chips from the previous night! We would do anything to make each other laugh in church. It was just dreadful; the Free Church Gaelic service in Kenneth Street. The English service was held in the Seminary.

In those days the Free Church Gaelic service was absolutely packed to the gunwales with hordes and hordes of people. One evening there was a group of us ran away and didn't go to church in the evening. We were reported to the teachers by my cousin Janet, one of the senior girls, who was also staying in the hostel. There were two teachers living there too, and half a dozen of us were called in to one of them, Don't ask me why this happened, but everybody got detention and had to write out chapters of the Bible. Then the teacher said to Chrissie MacKenzie and myself, "And as for you two, who should know better," because she knew that our people were very religious. So we were kept in longer for a further day, over and above the others, with an extra portion of the Bible to write out. That meant the minute we came home from school at a quarter past four we had to get it done before going to study, and we just never saw daylight.

At school we had some wonderful teachers. When you went to the Nicolson you were given a choice of Latin and French or Gaelic and French for the A and B classes. The A class was French and Latin, the B class was French and Gaelic; then there was the ones who didn't take any languages, the Cs and the Ds.

We worked on Gaelic. We were all already fluent, but we did all the literature and grammar. My first Gaelic teacher was 'Lofty' John MacArthur (everybody had nicknames) who was very funny. He was a composer of songs himself and he and his brother used to sing at concerts as Lofty and Chico. They would make up funny songs and they were well known. He was an amazing man. Lofty introduced us to all the Gaelic bards, and we could recite their works. We learned it until we had it on our tongues, "*tha e a agam air mo theanga*" by learning to recite. You had to learn screeds of everything, both English and Gaelic; and Bible. You had to learn it all because you didn't know who was going to be picked to stand up and deliver at any time. It's a wonderful technique because you don't forget, whereas if you just read it, it goes in one eye and out the other.

When I graduated to fourth year my Gaelic teacher was Alastair Urquhart, who was a wonderful teacher. He had a different sound to his Gaelic because he came from Ardnamurchan. It was through Alex Urquhart and the poetry that I got to know Scotland's geography. So I knew the place names in mainland Scotland before I ever went there and then couldn't wait to visit the locations. "Where's Ben Dorain?" I knew the place names and I was just over-awed by the country. But it's all because I was taught the poetry first. So my education had everything to do with what's happened ever since. By the end of our schooling he had introduced us to Irish Gaelic as well. We were so lucky.

One of my English teachers was Jean MacLean, and she was fey. She would forget what she was saying and she loved poetry so much she used to wander up and down reciting it to herself. A lot of people made fun of her, but I adored her, I really did. Maybe I liked her so much because there was poetry in myself and because I was slightly 'off-balance' too. She used to come to see me in Edinburgh, and I went to her funeral. It turned out she was the aunt of a friend who said to me, "What are you doing here?" I said, "She was my teacher." I wish to goodness I had kept her letters. But she made poetry so meaningful to us, absolutely. All the wonderful, wonderful poets and works such as 'The Ancient Mariner' and 'Morte d'Arthur', we knew them off by heart.

I eventually did my Higher English and Higher Gaelic, and one topic was Chaucer in English and Duncan Ban MacIntyre in Gaelic. I much preferred Chaucer to Shakespeare, because of the language. I found Shakespeare pretentious whereas I found Chaucer down to earth. (What a cheek!)

After Jean MacLean we had Mr Webster who was also the drama teacher. He was the one who brought drama alive. Every year we had a week-long event in the town hall, putting on shows, from the choir to the comedy and plays and everything, including the first stage play I was ever in. It was called 'The Dear Departed' and that was the first time my name appeared in the *Gazette*, for being in a play. My earliest theatrical credit. There are photographs of it and I can still remember everybody who was in it. I'm in touch with one of them, Martin Ure, who lives in America now.

I remember another one we did in which I was sitting in a frame in a long blue gown, and Christine MacDonald or 'Toby' as we called her, was dressed as an artist with white breeches, white ruff and a blue satin coat. She had her palette and her brush and she was painting me. Anyway, it was a terribly hard thing to do, to keep my composure because she was touching me with a paintbrush and I was supposed to be the picture, totally still. She was singing:

> *Dressed in your frock of blue brocade*
> *A rose upon its tiny shoe*
> *Lady in loveliness arrayed*
> *I'd like to dance with you*

I would step out of the frame and we would do a minuet together. Then I'd go back in and sit in the same position. It was a lovely piece. I don't know who wrote it.

In yet another show we did a dance, a Hungarian dance, and I had to borrow a boy's pair of trousers because I was playing the male. I remember his name was Philip MacLeod and I borrowed his short cords and galluses, the hat and things. You had to slap your heels behind you and it was all very, very funny. We were *so* lucky; we got all sorts of things to do. People tend to presume that in an island school the curriculum is narrow, and I only realised later how wide it was when I spoke to people who went to school in other places.

Miss Ross was our language teacher and she used to scream at me because I never used to remember French verbs, but she was lovely. She used to come and stay with me at Woodlands in Blair Atholl. There was another one whose name was Anne and we always called her 'Queen Anne', but I don't know why because the nicknames were passed down through the years. Quite often we didn't know what the nicknames meant or what they were for. I think it may have been because she taught history and French and may have talked of Queen Anne. One of the funniest incidents ever, which my friend Alec Murdo Maclean talked about for a very long time, was during the French class one morning, when a field mouse came in under the door and scampered around. Queen Anne jumped up on her chair and started screaming and we all started laughing until the boys shooed it out. I can't remember exactly what happened next, but in the afternoon we had a double period of maths. The teacher's name was Kenny and he came from somewhere round about Gairloch and he got called Cainey. Now he was wild, with no sympathy whatsoever, and when he got angry the blue veins would pulsate on the sides of his head. The girls decided that to cut the boredom towards the end of the first period the mouse was going to make a re-appearance. We were all to jump up in our seats and start screaming. Joan Morrison, who was sitting in the front row, was to give the signal, but when she turned round and I jumped up in my seat and started screaming not another soul moved. Everyone was supposed to do it, but nobody else had the nerve. I can still see him still, descending on me, with the pulsing veins. Everybody was in suppressed hysterics and spluttering. So I managed to say, "Please sir, I saw a mouse." And I'll never forget what he said in return: "You think if a mouse comes to school everything has to stop?"

Science was Miss Black, and Doc. I gave up maths and science in third year and took up art instead. My art teacher was Mr Chalmers, and there were only about six of us in the class, where we learned to do all sorts of things including craftwork as well as art, and art history. I tooled leather and made a handbag. We were very friendly, that section of us. We were a very close group because we were so small and I got the prize for art in my final year but haven't put a brush to paper since. It's something I always meant to take up again.

Of course, we also learned to cook and sew with a machine and we had to make dresses and do hand-stitches with scalloped edges and all sorts of things. That was overseen by Miss Calder.

It was great, and there were so many characters around. I was also in the Guides for a while and then in the Rangers and I loved it. Our Ranger captain was Ann Urquhart, who later became a Ross and Cromarty councillor and then Lord Lieutenant. At her farewell speech at the council meeting at Dingwall she was referred to as ex-councillor Urquhart, ex-Lord Lieutenant, ex-this and ex-that and she got up and said, "Well one thing's certain, I'm the 'exiest' woman here."

The Rangers used to plant flowers in pots in Perceval Square in the springtime and they'd do what we would call community work now. I used to go on a Sunday morning to this old woman and make a cup of tea for her but it was dreadful. Nobody should have been allowed to do that. She was in great poverty and surrounded by dirt. She looked forward to me coming and I liked going, but she had two pet rats called Durlo and Barney. I don't know if they actually existed because I never saw them, but she was always talking to them. She lived in a close behind a bakery shop. I don't know if she had any relatives, and I can't remember why I stopped going, whether she was taken away to hospital or what, but I don't think she would have been left like that today. At that time there were no carers or anything, just neighbours, although that was not always a bad thing. Neighbours looked after each other a lot more than they do now.

The Guides and Rangers activities were always conducted in English. We were on parade often, for Armistice Day and things like that, along with the Brownies and Guides, the Scouts and the Cubs. One event with the Rangers changed my life. It was when the royal yacht *Britannia* came to Stornoway, and I was in my last year at school. The Rangers were in the guard of honour when she came alongside. So there were the Brownies, the Guides, the Scouts, and, because of my height or something, I happened to be the first Ranger in the line. The Duke of Edinburgh spoke to me, although I don't even remember what he said.

There was to be an open-air dance in Stornoway that night but was I allowed to stay for it? Absolutely not! I was so angry. I was furious that all my friends were staying over for it and I had to go home to Marvig because it was a Saturday. I came home on the boat, which sailed in the wake of the Britannia and it broke my heart to leave my friends on the pier. Our house was quite a long bit from the shore, and as soon as I appeared by my Auntie Peggy's house, my mother started shouting, "Get out of that nonsense clothes you're wearing [the uniform] and get over to Calbost to help your brother put nets over the hay before the Sabbath." I was so angry that I went in, pulled off my things, put on some old clothes and went out to our shed which was full of bicycles and taking one put a net on the handlebars and set off on the two miles to Calbost.

I was going down a hill and I went to put the brakes on but there were none. I went right over the handlebars into a rock. I walked the remaining mile and worked, still angry and not realising how badly hurt I was. It was dark when we finished, and as we were walking back home Donald said, "I thought you'd bring a bike." I said, "I did." And when we got to the place, there was the bike in two bits. And he looked at me and saw for the first time that I had a huge cut on my forehead, and my hands had no skin on them and they had got the grass dye in them by this time. I was damned if I was going to say anything.

When we got into the house I passed out. And my mother said, "That's what you get. It's your own fault. That's what you get, for losing your temper". A couple of months later, my knee gave way and I had to get fluid taken off it regularly. I had been high jump champion at the Nicolson but my knee was gone. When I fell off the bicycle a chip had come off my patella and dislodged the cartilage and I still have the scar to prove it. So that is why I know I should never lose my temper and never complain. It's always my own fault!

ᗣ

Our weekends in Stornoway were always taken up. We had to do our washing on Friday nights and dry it on the heating pipes before ironing it on Saturday morning using heavy, heavy irons. There was a circular range for flat irons and they cooled very quickly, so you took one out and then another. Health and safety was not a consideration. We had to wear gym frocks that were all pleated, so all that had to be done every week too.

Usually we went up to the gym and played badminton on Saturday afternoon, and perhaps go to the pictures at night, because we didn't have to study. There was a shop called TB MacAulay's that did clothes, wool and that kind of thing and at that time they were selling locally made scarves by post. My cousin Mina worked there and I would go in after school and see what there was to do. Sometimes there would be a dozen parcels of scarves going away, so I started doing the post for five shillings a week but on Saturday I did all the messages for Kirsty MacAulay so I made a little more pocket money.

Then there was the annual football team outing, that everybody wanted to go on. The school team went on a trip to Garry Sands at

Tolsta every summer. The sixth year boys went with the team but you always hoped that somebody would invite you along. It had to be by invitation so you always tried to snuggle up to someone who was in the team a few weeks beforehand, whether you liked him or not! That was a great day out. We used to have picnics and games. All supervised, of course. There was no room for any kind of hanky-panky at either the school or the hostel because everything was supervised.

We used to have social events at school. We had class socials, but then we would also have a social with the boys' hostel when we used to dance. Everybody could dance. We danced anything and everything but it was before the era of the twist. We had a mixture: quickstep and tango and eightsome reels and we always had a band. In the hostel we had a big record player, and if you asked nicely it would be brought in to the laundry on Saturday morning, and we would play the pop stars of the time; *Sipping Soda through a Straw* and *She Wears Red Feathers* and *A Hula Hula Skirt* and some Scottish music as well, like Jimmy Shand.

Sometimes I would go up and stay with my aunty at the weekends, to get out of the hostel, and then I would go to a dance at the YM. Christine 'Toby' and I would dress up and go to the YM dances.

Then there was one big dance, which I think was a summer ball in the town hall. You could be excused from the hostel if it was a reasonable, legitimate thing such as that. Kirsty MacAulay, of the family I used to post the parcels for, didn't want to go by herself so she asked if I would go with her. I was seventeen then and had no suitable clothes, so I went up to their house, which was above the shop. I wore a copper taffeta frock with a full skirt, and it was absolutely gorgeous, It was one of Kirsty's own I think, and when Kirsty and myself came downstairs Mrs MacAulay looked at me and said, "You need something else," and she went and got a necklace of moonstones. When she put them round my neck I thought I was the Queen of Sheba. I looked amazing. I can't remember what I had on my feet, but I couldn't have had stylish shoes back then. That was my first ball and it was wonderful. And of course, they put Slipperene on the floor in those days and everybody glided along in the waltzes and quicksteps and tangos and sambas. That was a really, really great night.

I remember being terribly, terribly envious one night of Mairi Murray, as her father was taking her to a dance. I was so envious of Mairi, having a father who took her, for if my own had been alive, I was sure I would have been going to a dance with him too.

In terms of music there must have been a local Mod, but I never sang in it as I had to leave the choir. However we used to do action songs in school and in the hostel as well. By action songs I mean a musical play in Gaelic. There would be a story through it, with songs. These were taught by a wonderful singing teacher called Annie MacKenzie. She was from Point and had been a missionary and she had a bad limp, but she is well known. Mr Short took us for classical music when we learned different things. Although singing English songs meant nothing to me whatsoever, it was balanced by Annie MacKenzie who coached us in all the traditional stuff as well as the action songs.

All we listened to on the radio was the news, piping, Scottish dance music and 'The MacFlannels'. Everything was very Scottish, but we used to get opera and things in Stornoway too. We went with the school or hostel and we were ushered in. I can still remember one woman who she looked as if she was wearing velvet curtains and she was singing *The Blacksmith*. I mimicked her for ages but it did not appeal to me. Mr Short used to drum the last flat or the last sharp into us but I was never interested in classical music at all. I love listening to it now, but we used to sight read tonic sol-fa and do scales which I found off putting. So, we had the two extremes of music in class, with Annie MacKenzie and Mr Short.

The songs I brought to Edinburgh were just part of growing up; you absorbed them. I don't know how but everybody knew the songs, the local songs, and we had psalms morning and night, but they also played the accordion and pipes, so there wasn't any puritanical religious thing about music making. There used to be concerts in the school or in the village, and people went there and sang. So you'd hear the old songs a lot. We danced too, even in the village school, where there were sixteen of us. We all learned to dance and always danced in the porch if it was raining outside. To me, singing and dancing were just absorbed. I don't remember learning any of it. It was part of the evolution of growing up.

Rock and roll hadn't come in when I was at school. It started around 1957. Although there were records in the hostel we did not have transistor radios or television. However we somehow knew all the latest things that were going on from somewhere or other. We could go into a shop as there were a couple that sold records and all sorts of bits and pieces.

ೞ

My first visit to the mainland was when I went to Glasgow for a few days. I was still at school, and I was bridesmaid at my sister's wedding. I had said that I wanted to go to a proper theatre, that was the only thing I wanted to do and someone I knew, Compton MacLeod, who was at university at Glasgow, said he'd take me while I was there. So the day after the wedding he came to my cousin's house and took me to the theatre. I was overawed by the place but it was not to my taste. I had wanted to see a play, but this was a variety show with women with fat thighs high-kicking and comics. I knew then that that wasn't my idea of theatre and I've never liked that sort of thing. However, it was my first visit to a *real* theatre, all red plush upholstery and gold leaf. It was an experience, although not my artistic cup of tea.

After my Highers I left school. My sister in Dumfriesshire was expecting a baby so I spent the summer there with her, helping out. I suppose I had what's known now as a gap year. So in a way, I was eased into the thought and reality of mainland life. I was excited but I was not apprehensive about going because I knew so much about it from other people.

Chapter 4

To the Mainland

I'M SURE it was living with my father's illness which made me wish to work in hospitals in some way. But after his death, I couldn't bear injections. I don't mind getting them myself, but I can't bear to see anybody else getting injections; just a throwback I suppose. But I was very, very good at art, craft and creative stuff, and somebody told me about occupational therapy, so I applied and I got an interview.

So I went on the ferry and my sister Jessie, who lived in Moffat at the time with her husband the vet, had my suit ready for me for the interview. I had only been away once before, to be Jessie's bridesmaid. The interview was at the Astley Ainslie hospital, which is where the occupational therapy training place was, and hundreds of girls applied there every year. I was wearing a second hand coat and my mother's overshoes on top of my shoes, and Jessie had my suit all ready in Moffat. But there was a howling hurricane and the boat didn't sail, so I had to send a telegram saying, "Storm-bound, possibly late for interview."

The boat left the next day, with only seven of us, and all the men were saying, "It's all right, we'll look after you," and I was the only one who wasn't sea-sick. When the boat arrived in Mallaig, I had to get a train to Glasgow, but we had to change at Cowlairs in order to get to Edinburgh. So I got on the train at Cowlairs, with no idea where I was going, except that I had to go to the Astley Ainslie Hospital. A man and his mother started chatting to me. At this time I was still wearing my mother's overshoes, I'd lost a button off my coat, I couldn't get to Moffat for my posh clothes, and I had my portfolio with pages of drawings. Anyway, when we got off at Waverley, this couple took me in hand. There was some family member meeting them and they insisted on driving me to the Astley Ainslie. They wouldn't let me out of the car until they found the right department and the person in charge of that department. To this day I don't know who they were and I hadn't the nous to ask them. I'm sure I thanked them, but I'd been away from home for two and a half days and had had no sleep. I went in to face the people on the interview board, and there I was, shauchling in wearing a coat without a button, like something the cat dragged in.

So that's how I got there, and they just started laughing at me. There were five or six of them round a table. They just looked at my drawings and I got a letter the following week saying I'd been accepted, one of only thirty-two out of three hundred.

After that I spent the summer in Moffat. My sister was expecting a baby at the time, so I went down to be with her. She already had one child who was not quite a year old. I worked in a guesthouse for two wonderful, matronly sisters. Everything was so precise, and I suppose that's where I first picked up how to serve dinner and afternoon tea and starch the napkins and silver service and all that sort of thing. I suppose this was the beginning of the road to Blair Atholl, the beginning of my education in catering. I also made lifelong friends there; the Lockhart family round the corner. I'm still in touch with Sheila and her husband.

We used to have dances every Friday night in the town hall or in Wamphray, one of the local villages and they had wonderful bands.

We used to buy material and make circular skirts; you just spread the material out and made a hole in the middle to fit your waist and put a waistband and a hem on it. And stiff petticoats and white, blancoed high heels, and go down to the town hall and dance the night away. I was nineteen. It was a wonderful, totally carefree time before my studies began.

At that time there was a ban on Sunday drinking unless you drove three miles – *bona fide* travellers – so all the farmers came from Dumfries and round about to Moffat House Hotel for dinner. David, my brother-in-law, who was the vet, couldn't always go so I often went instead, because I didn't drink. So I met a lot of interesting Dumfriesshire farmers and their wives. It was an education for me and total immersion in a different culture.

There was another Lewis family there who had come to work in Moffat as waitresses from school in Tolsta, so I wasn't completely isolated from the language. I also met a wonderful guy called Arthur Rankin who became very important in education in Scotland. His mother made me a dress for my 21st birthday.

☙

So the day came when I had to leave for the Astley Ainslie – properly dressed up this time – and I was terribly nervous. The occupational therapy hostel was at 12 Church Hill, a huge big house, and the first person I met was a girl of about my own age who came bouncing down the stairs and said, " Where do you come from? I come from Hong Kong. What does your father do?

Mine's in shipping." That was my introduction, and when all the other girls arrived some of them were immaculately dressed, they had all gone to private girls' schools, and they all knew each other's brothers, who played rugger and that sort of thing. It seemed as if everybody else had been to boarding school. They were very posh, with loads of money, and somebody's brother was at Gordonstoun. It was very alien to me and it was then that I first became conscious of class, although there had been a bit of snobbery at Stornoway as well, such as the people next door to us studying French and Latin who were snooty because we were doing Gaelic instead. There was a bit of that, and you were always aware of the people with flash cars coming in from the shooting estates. But it was the first time I'd lived among it.

I just felt so totally out of it until a couple of evenings later. Our baths were in cubicles without a top to them, I think with three baths to a room, and this night I was homesick as anything. I was lying in the bath, and someone started singing *An t-Eilean Muileach*, 'The Isle of Mull', and I joined in and we both said, "Who's that?" And a voice said, "I'm Morven". I said, "I'm Dolina," and we stood on the edges of our baths and put our soapy hands to each other over the top. She was Morven Cameron, whose father came from Mull and was a baker in Ayr. Morven and I became great friends. She died four years ago.

My first roommate was Lorna Sim, who came from Coleraine. Her father was a vet there, so we had a common thing, what with David being a vet in Moffat. The last time I met Lorna was at Morven's funeral. Anyway I didn't know the difference between Northern Ireland and Eire; I knew there was a difference but didn't understand the politics of it. So she explained a lot of that to me and that was another bit of knowledge which I wouldn't have got in Stornoway.

On Fridays my friend Christine stayed in the YWCA in Palmerston Place. She was doing speech therapy, so she met an awful lot of students that we didn't meet, except on Fridays when we went for anatomy to the medical school in Teviot Place. We used to pass lots of medical students on our way, so we all dressed to kill on Friday mornings. That's an exaggeration but Christine met a lot of people and it was through her that I got involved in folk singing.

ை

At the end of my first year I went back to Moffat to work at the Auchen Castle Hotel. That was wonderful. It was a huge hotel which is still there. You had to leave Moffat, go on to the Beattock Road and up a hill; you can still see it from the train, before you come to Beattock Summit. I can't remember the name of the proprietor, but he was very funny.

That's where I had my education, really, or another side of my education, because the chef was a big brute of a man called Bob, who had been a ship's chef. He was huge and we were terrified of him. There were two waiters; one was called Kenny, and there was also a Polish man called John, who was immaculate in black bow tie and tails every night as head waiter. I remember one night singing away in the kitchen while I was queuing for the chef to give me an order. The dining room was very quiet that night and a couple asked where the music was coming from. Somebody said it was me, so I had to go and sing to them. That was the only time I sang down in Moffat – apart from when my sister and brother-in-law had parties.

There was so much intrigue going on between the staff, and of course I was terribly naive and didn't realise that affairs were going on. They were very kind and didn't involve me in any of it, but I was nosy enough to find out

Because I was a student and spoke well, with a very Highland accent, I got twice as many tips as anybody else. But after two or three weeks, suddenly we had to pool the tips. We only got paid something like three pounds a week, and you had to be on call, and because I lived in the village, if there was a rush they would just phone up and somebody would come for me and I just had to work. But I really loved it.

‌ CR

Although I had worked hard at college I failed anatomy. I had to take a re-sit but I failed it and lost my grant, because in those days if you failed you lost your support. My sister came in one day with the letter from the college. I opened it and burst into tears as did she and we just hugged each other and thought, 'what to do, what to do, what to do?' It was a terrible shock, and when I finished at Auchen Castle I went back home. My tutors at Astley Ainslie were terribly disappointed, because I'd come very near the top in psychology and all the crafts – weaving and basket making, you name it. I got a tremendously sympathetic letter from the staff. They were really disappointed, but they couldn't do anything about it or finance my stay. So there I was, back home in Lewis, very depressed, when they got in touch with me about the occupational centre in Fife which was looking for staff, suggesting that it would suit me. So I interviewed for that and got the job.

I often wonder what would have happened if I had passed the anatomy exam. I suspect I would have been bored out of my head, because shortly after that occupational therapists stopped doing what we were trained for. In those days people went for convalescence, and the reason for occupational therapy was to help recovering and disabled people use and strengthen their limbs by pulling straw, weaving and other activities. But that's all gone now. We were taught to make sea grass stools and learned woodwork and such like. We used to go to Torphichen Street School for woodwork once a week. We learned how to fume oak and I wove tartan and made all sorts of wonderful tooled leather things. The Astley Ainslie is still a convalescent hospital, but occupational therapists now teach patients how to walk and make sure their homes have got the correct facilities like railings and that sort of thing. It's changed dramatically and I don't know if I would have enjoyed that part of it as much as the part that I had been trained for. But the singing had taken over by then anyway and it had awoken an interest in tradition, learning about other people's cultures and broadening my mind. I didn't know *what* was waiting for me anywhere, but that was to be another step on my journey.

Chapter 5

A Sojourn in Fife

I STARTED work in Fife in an occupational centre for what we then called mentally handicapped children, nowadays known as special needs.

There were five occupational centres in Fife at that time to cater for the number of children with such difficulties. There was still much poverty and inadequate housing. The mining industry was collapsing and people had little money. Children used to go about the bings picking up coal for their families. In the past, if you had anything to do with the mines you got so many hundredweight of coal free, but that had largely stopped. It was the first time I had seen real poverty.

The occupational centre was in Lochgelly, and took in children from the adjoining mining communities of Cowdenbeath, Lochore and Ballingray. There happened to be a couple from home living in Lochgelly, Calum-na-Toff from Gravir and his wife Mairead Ishbel-Fhionnlaigh from Marvig, so I stayed with them and their lovely children until I found lodgings with a Mrs McKinlay in Birnie Street.

It was around that time that I met Lawrence Daly (who became national secretary of the National Union of Mineworkers from 1968 to 1984 and founder of the Fife Socialist League). I used to babysit for him. His children were all named after place names; Rannoch, Kerren, Cavan, Morven and Shannon. He had an English wife, who spoke with an English/Lochgelly accent; "Rennoch, come ben the hoose."

Lawrence was an incredible singer and on Wednesday afternoons, he and I used to do old folks' clubs in Cowdenbeath and Cardenden, and on Sunday nights we would do the British Legion. And he sang always *The Star of the County Down* and *Dear Old Donegal.* I remember one night we were singing in the British Legion (I hadn't sung there before because I usually went back to Edinburgh at weekends) and Lawrence introduced me and I sang a Gaelic song. The place was absolutely stunned and not very appreciative at all. Then the MC said, "Yous can all say that you heard something different the night ... and now for wir ain Jeannie." And she started singing *I'll Take You Home Again Kathleen* and they returned to happiness after that.

When there was an exodus from the Communist Party following Soviet suppression of the 1956 Hungarian uprising, Lawrence helped form the Fife Socialist League with his uncle. Scottish Nationalism had little presence in industrial Fife, and for years the Labour Party was not very strong, which allowed the emergence of the League as an alternative to Labour. Few of them had formal education, but they were so well read. My first fundraising escapade for them was on a Saturday in Ballingray, and apart from singing and helping, I had to auction what could have been an illicit copy of 'Lady Chatterley's Lover', which had been banned in Britain by the Censor. We made about fifty quid on it – everybody wanted to read it.

At the same time there were the two famous brothers, Abe and Alex Moffat (both presidents of the NUM in Scotland). They came to hear me sing in Edinburgh at the Waverley bar one night, and I remember that someone was being snobbish to the miners and said something, and one of the Moffats replied, "I'll have you know that I went to a public school ... Cowdenbeath Public School." He had twice the knowledge and experience of the student who was baiting him.

So folk like Abe and Alex Moffat were around, but I was totally unaware in those days of what it was all about politically. I was just there to provide entertainment, because there were no folksingers around then. Things were just starting to move from the *Bonnie Wee Jeannie McCall* sort of thing to traditional folk music. There was also Irish music coming across, and at that time I was only vaguely aware of Irish politics. It was through hearing their songs that I became aware of the Troubles and began to understand the possible power of the people.

My landlady in Birnie Street had great philosophical advice for everything, "What's for you'll no go by you". It was the first time I ever heard that expression and I still can't bear to hear it. She was in a kind of women's freemasonry, the 'Eastern Star' and her comment about every meeting seemed to be, "Oh the steak pie wasnae as good as last week."

I liked cheese and used to buy it every week and she put it in the coal cellar outside because it stank the house out. In time I became friendly with the daughter of her neighbour across the road and she invited me and Robin [Gray] to a party just outside Dunfermline. John Watt and his then wife, Ann, were at the party, and he had never ever heard a folk song before. He was mesmerised with Robin's playing and our singing. John went on to become a shining light on the folk scene and composed many songs that will be sung for ever more, such as *The Keltie Clippy* and *Pittenweem Joe*.

So that's how the Dunfermline Folk Song Society started back in 1961. It was in Chalmers Street and they called it the Dunfermline Howff, because the Edinburgh Howff was ongoing at the time.

I also started a junior Gaelic choir in Dunfermline, and I took them all through to Edinburgh to sing in a ceilidh one time; about eight or ten little children, some of them children of Gaelic-speakers living in Fife. There was a girl living there from Sutherland who was a native speaker and there were quite a few families from the islands, where the mothers had gone to work in local hotels and had married and stayed on.

☙

Among the children I worked within the occupational centre was Jimmy, who was adopted by a miner's family. He could not control the spasms in his hands; he must have had cerebral palsy, but we didn't know that at the time. After about two weeks I got him to concentrate enough to put a bead on a lace. So I sent him home with a few beads and a shoe lace, and I got a letter back from his father, saying they never thought they would see this happen, and God bless you.

Every Friday afternoon they had to perform, but some of them were too shy, so I got a piece of plywood and a fretsaw and made the outline of a television set – just a frame with knobs – and put it on the table in front of them. Television was just becoming available then, so I would get one of them to 'turn on the television', and perform in front of the class. Normally they wouldn't do anything in front of the class, but pretending to be on television was different, and the response was amazing.

There was another boy called Jimmy, from Cowdenbeath, who had Down's Syndrome and he was huge for his age. He was fourteen and could be quite violent. His mother came one Monday, and said, "Do you speak a different language or something?" And I said that I spoke Gaelic, why? And she said, "Well we had a family wedding at the weekend, and everybody was doing their party pieces. And suddenly Jimmy, who had never done anything like it before, got up to do his party piece and went, '*A hum and a hi and a ho* … Miss Maclennan, haw haw.'" So the next time I saw him I said to him, "Jimmy, what did you do at the weekend?" and he laughed and repeated the imitation.

That was another big breakthrough for a family, but it was this television that did it. I had done woodwork when I was doing occupational therapy and had made mortise and tenon joints, so I knew all about it, and this was just a simple cut-out frame, but it worked.

The occupational centre was a brand new building, down in the field beside Lochgelly Secondary, and in the fifties these new buildings had heating gratings on the walls, at head height. I got a cold sore and it spread, right across my face, because some of the children were full of infections and I think because of the heating. It would clear up at the weekend but then when I got back, by Tuesday it was all over me again. I got *so* depressed about it, and I went to the doctor, who gave me some pills, which made me feel absolutely wonderful. I came back to Edinburgh, and Robin commented on how well I looked. I said, "Oh I've never felt so good in all my life. Dr Blue gave me those pills." Robin looked at them and he just opened the Aga and threw them in. I was on purple hearts – three a day. Robin was studying dentistry and had some medical knowledge. No wonder I felt so wonderful. That was my one and only excursion into taking barbiturates.

Eventually I had to leave, because my face just wouldn't heal, and that was the end of my work in the Kingdom and the Fife Socialist League, but I kept in touch with Lawrence. He was down the mines at the time, but he became Joe Gormley's second-in-command in the NUM.

During that time I also made friends with Russell Johnston, later Lord Russell Johnston, Liberal MP for Inverness, who was teaching at Lochgelly Secondary School, as was one of my good friends, Meg Doig, who is godmother to one of my daughters. On Fridays we'd get the train to Edinburgh together and we saw the Forth Road Bridge as it was being built, watching it gradually rise out of the Firth.

I was in Fife for two years or more, but I came back to Edinburgh and started dental nursing, with Gordon Watt in Gilmore Place. I had to find a job and I could no longer work with the children because of my health, so I looked in the *Evening News,* and saw, 'Dental nurse needed.' I went for the interview and got the job. I really enjoyed my time with Gordon, who was a wonderful man. He lived out at Barnton and eventually he and his wife and daughter emigrated to South Africa.

When I first came back to Edinburgh I stayed with Hamish Henderson and his wife Kätzel for two or three weeks. Earlier on in Edinburgh, through Hamish, I'd met an American called Bobby Botsford who was part of the scene and a great friend of Hamish's. He had a flat at 19 Bristo Place, above Napier's the herbalist. I was going to have the use of the flat but I stayed with Hamish because Roy Guest (about whom more later) was still staying there.

Hamish and Kätzel were keen for me to stay with them as long as possible but I wanted to get into my own flat – Bobby's flat. I paid rent for it, not to Bobby but to an agency he had looking after it, all above board. I went over one lunchtime and there was a fire engine there and burning rubbish outside. Everybody thought it was people with a grievance at Roy Guest, but it eventually transpired that it wasn't that at all. The tale was recalled more than a decade later by Hamish Henderson, chronicling the Edinburgh folk scene in *Sandy Bell's Broadsheet*, 16 March, 1974:

> After lunch Dolly and I decided to go and have a clear look at the ruin and (fortifying ourselves with a drink or two on the way) we returned to Bristo Place, passed the smouldering wreckage on the pavement and started to climb the stair.
>
> On the way up we met Donny MacDonald, a policeman from near Oban, who was coming down. Dolly said, 'So they've got it at last,' and the bold Donny replied, 'It's not yours this time!'
>
> And right enough, we found upstairs that Dolly's flat was untouched – the smoking ruin was the flat opposite!
>
> Its door was wide open, and inside we could see two policemen taking a statement from the inmate, an old woman. And then it all came out.
>
> The fire-raiser, in all cases, had been this same old screwball who lived across the way. Hopelessly behind with the rent, she had got the idea into her head that she might be able to move into Roy's flat when it was empty, and seeing it occupied by what she took to be a tribe of hirsute, glazed-eyed hippies, she hit on the idea of scaring them out by fire-raising.

Finally, realising that the new inmate was resolved to hold the fort, she had made the best of a bad job and set fire to her own flat – the interior of which looked like something out of the blitz: hundreds of old jam jars, opened tins, empty milk bottles and miscellaneous hoarded paraphernalia of every description. In the middle of the floor of the living room lay four partly burned car tyres.

So, the mystery, which had been alarming enough in its time, had a rather pathetic ending ...

In a later article in the *Broadsheet,* Hamish would describe these and other goings-on at the Bristo Place flat as, 'a mixture of grand guignol, the Marx brothers and Edgar Allan Poe'.

When it was eventually all sorted out and I moved in, I just put a sheet of hardboard over where the floor was burned. All sorts of people came to stay with me while I was there. It was pretty basic but I tried to make it as nice as possible.

ରେ

One of the funniest stories from my dental nursing days – every Friday afternoon at the surgery a certain doctor used to come to administer gas for extractions. He brought his gas cylinders and, strangely enough, we all used to have fits of the giggles on Friday afternoons without ever realising why. We just thought it was that Friday feeling, but the gas must have been leaking. He was subsequently struck off as an anaesthetist.

We used to go to the restaurant next to Sandy Bell's bar, my friend Mary Sandilands and I, and have tea on Fridays – pay day – and then it was on to the Waverley for me. So Friday nights were always wonderful, because we were high.

I remember a particular Friday patient who was having all his teeth out. When the dentist finished he'd go next door for a coffee or a cigarette and we'd do the tidying up. I was left with this huge man, holding a kidney basin under his chin and slapping his cheeks to bring him round, and saying, "Spit into the basin, come on." He opened his eyes and looked at me and I said, "That's good, spit into the basin." The wash-hand basin was about six feet away and he aimed at it with a mouthful of blood, not realising I had the basin under his chin. Of course he didn't have teeth anymore and it sprayed all over me and the surgery.

It used to be quite embarrassing for me on Friday afternoons – because I was quite young then – as I had to tell gentlemen to go upstairs to the toilet first, because quite often they could have a bladder accident under the gas.

I used to walk all the way down from Bristo Place to the surgery in Gilmore Place and I was nearly always running because it would be five to nine. There was a policeman on duty at Tollcross, before they had traffic lights there, and he got to know me in my rush, so he used to stop the traffic for me, and shout, "C'mon Pixie. You'll make it!" because my hair was very short then.

It was a happy time, even though for a time I was very broken hearted after Robin and I split up. Of course I was working with adults again after those two years of working with children. My health been so bad working with them, and when you're in your early twenties, if you've cold sores from ear to ear, the depression is just awful. So I think changing my job and environment, having my own flat instead of my cheese being put into the coal cellar and being able to cook for myself and have friends round all helped. And before long, 19 Bristo Place became a focal point for visiting musicians.

Chapter 6

Folksinger

How does one become a folk singer? It all started after I met Stuart MacGregor at a party in April 1958. I had been invited to a dance at a castle outside Edinburgh by a second-year medic and had agreed to go. I'd been to a few posh dances locally while working in Auchen Castle Hotel and my sister had bought me an amazing frock. It was white cotton, with sprigs and flowers and had a little bolero. Of course, it was the time of full skirts and high heels, so when a chap invited me a dance at a place called Rosslyn Castle I knew just what to wear. However, when I arrived I saw that everyone else was in casual trousers (there were no jeans then) and sitting on bales of straw. It was a barn dance! I was mortified, or to quote what my actor friend Roy Hanlon used to say, "*Mor-ti-fied!*" So I just jumped on a bus back into town and I never saw my medic escort again.

That same evening Christine Fletcher, my friend from Stornoway, had been invited to a party in the fashionable West End of the city, at the house of Robin Scott-Moffat, an older man about town and part of the Edinburgh social scene. So I went with Christine to that party.

We had not been there long when a dental student from Uist came into the kitchen and asked if anybody could sing. Christine said, "Doli sings" and the lad responded, "Well, sing then!" We were so green. I sang and he said, "Stop, don't do anything more till I get MacGregor." After I'd stopped this guy Stuart MacGregor came into the room. I sang again and Stuart said, "Don't let Henderson get a hold of her," whereupon another big man came in. Stuart was joking of course, for it turned out that was the same night that he, Hamish Henderson and others had inaugurated the Edinburgh University Folksong Society. Tim Neat covers this in his biography of Hamish where he quotes me:

> ... there he was. And he came towards me with these great arms high above his head and he encloaked me – and a feeling of pure benevolence came on me. It was like a blessing that has stayed with me till this day. And there was Stuart, announcing that the Edinburgh University Folk Club had made its first great discovery!

So, that's how it all started. I became the sort of *pet* of the new folk music scene in Edinburgh, largely because of my youth, my innocence and because I may have represented something authentic and of another world. Hamish told Tim that he recalled me arriving, "like a shepherdess, trailing these songs of gold from ancient times".

I was soon meeting musicians, poets, writers and artists. I was naive in so many ways but I did have an inquiring attitude and I learned to say, "I don't know about that; tell me." I think at first I was embarrassed at my lack of street wisdom and I could not see until recently that I must have had something that was different and interesting and why Anne Lorne Gillies has written of me as, "the darling of the folk revival in Edinburgh".

So, having met Hamish Henderson at that party I was soon up at the University of Edinburgh's School of Scottish Studies, recording my versions of traditional Gaelic songs. I see from the archive, now available on the Tobar an Dualchais website, that I gave him seven items in 1958 and others in subsequent years:

> Riobanan Rìomhach Màiri/Far am bi mi fhèin 's ann a bhios mo dhòchas/Hai O Haiream Chunna' Mise A-raoir Thu/Rionnag anns an Oidhche Fhrasaich
>
> Hi Horò 's na hòro eile
>
> Och Nan Och Tha Mi Fo Mhulad
>
> Òran Chaluim Sgàire
>
> Hug Oireann òro gur Toigh Leam Fhìn Thu
>
> Tha mi Duilich, Duilich, Duilich
>
> Chan eil Mo Leannan ann an Seo

My musical style was quite different to what most other Gaelic singers were offering in and around Edinburgh at the time. The traditional singers Kitty and Marietta Macleod had left by then and Flora MacNeill had returned to Barra before I arrived. Some Gaelic singers sang in a trained kind of style that was acceptable at the National Mod, but not on the folk scene. Other like Annag MacLeod and Agnes MacLennan sang traditional songs at the Saturday ceilidhs in the West End Hotel but, again, not on the folk scene. Then you had the wonderful voices of Joan MacKenzie and Calum Kennedy, who sang in the theatre and at big concerts, but also not considered folk.

In terms of the revival, Morag MacLeod has recalled that, "Gaelic was not part of the interest in folk groups that came about in the mid-1950s ... Folksong societies heard too little of Gaelic singing of the authentic traditional type for its members to be able to judge it with any degree of discrimination."

But those early days in Edinburgh were really fantastic. It was the very beginning of things happening, and I remember the first concerts that Hamish organised. They were lunchtime affairs at the Gartshore Hall on George Street in August 1958, during the Festival. Jeannie Robertson was involved, and a youthful Robin Hall. The *Glasgow Herald* rightly noted that Jeannie's singing of the *Battle of Harlaw* and *My Son David*, "had tremendous power and an extraordinary evocation of the Scottish past" and kindly added:

> It says much for Dolina Maclennan, from Lewis, and Robin Hall, from Glasgow, that these young singers are not altogether overshadowed by their fellow artists. Both give a good account of themselves with songs from their respective home backgrounds.

Hamish had started similar gatherings with Joan Littlewood some years earlier and had built up a circle of enthusiasts. So I was in with that crowd right at the beginning. Through him I was introduced to Ella and Simon Ward and so many others. Hamish encouraged Robin Hall too as he was very interested in traditional songs. This was before he and Jimmie MacGregor became household names on television and moved to London.

My main interest was the traditional side epitomised by Jeannie Robertson. I met Jeannie right at the beginning, learned a few songs from her and was soon comfortable singing them. We became great friends and I used to visit her and her husband in Aberdeen where they lived. I also got to know the great singer Jimmy MacBeath, who just came and went; he was a man of the road. I don't think he actually tramped although he might have done at one time. When he started out on the folk circuit, he couldn't believe that anybody would pay him for singing *Tramps and Hawkers* and those wonderful songs. Nobody could touch him for singing them. He'd take up the whole stage, and he wore shauchly clothes, but he was a darling.

Jeannie was the major figure, and she always wore a red cardigan, red plastic earrings, had hair all over the place and a wonderful face. I remember when my daughter Mary was born, I took her over to Hamish's where Jeannie was staying, for her to see the newborn. She took the baby into her arms, looked at her and said, "Aye, this yin's been here afower."

Jeannie was once at a Lord Provost's reception in the City Chambers during the Edinburgh Festival, and there was a Highland type with a kilt on who made a snide remark in Gaelic, Well, Jeannie said nothing but afterwards she recounted to me what happened next. Jeannie said, "He took one look at me and said, 'I see we've got tinkers in the camp tonight'. But he didnae ken that I kent the Gaelic." She didn't know it all that well either but she understood quite a bit of it. She went on, "I kent that he'd come and speak to me and be awfu' polite, so when he came over, I said, 'You're a Highlander?' And he says, 'Aye.' So I says, 'If you're a Hielander, how do you no ken that it wasn't a tinker what put the nose on you.'" Some people were like that about travellers and the traditional ways. Some of those Gaelic folk were arrogant as hell, and that's what happened with Jeannie, but it's a nice story.

There was really just the Folksong Society at Edinburgh University then. Hamish and Stuart had started it that night in April 1958, and it soon became a riot of hectic activity. A year later there were over a hundred members and I was singing along with Stuart, Robin Gray, Ella Ward and others. When I succeeded Stuart as president of the society after he left for National Service, I used to do all sorts of things to generate interest. I remember going round the common room in the university's Old Quad and speaking to the students there, asking what country they came from. I got them all together for an evening and they sang their own countries' songs. That was the first ever international folksong concert in Edinburgh, a forerunner of the kind of gatherings that became quite common later. That was back in 1959. Then one night a new girl came and sang. I recently found my notebook from the time, which says, 'New girl, Jean Redpath … Sounds promising.' Patronising bitch that I was! But she herself was very shy, having only just come over from Leven in Fife. Yes, it was a very, very interesting time.

Robin Gray, singer and guitarist, started going out with Christine Fletcher at first, but soon he and I started singing together. We had a residency at the Waverley Bar, in St Mary's Street, and sang together for more than three years. So, Robin and I were really the first pub folksingers in Edinburgh. There wasn't any other live folk music going on in the city pubs at that time. Why the Waverley? Because Ian Walker, the proprietor, wanted music there and he was willing to give it a try in his upstairs lounge. Somebody had heard Robin and myself and suggested us to him and he got in touch. So we started singing there, and I was terrified in case they heard at home that I was singing in a pub. But after a while it just became accepted. They tried it on Saturdays to begin with and we got £3 between us for three hours' performing, singing in Gaelic and in English.

So many people have said that those nights in the Waverley were the start of their awareness of Gaelic. For instance, the late Alan McCartney MEP told me years later that it was hearing me singing there that got him interested in the language. Up till then the only Gaelic singing that non-Gaels heard was Mod-type singing which could sound very stylised. There was only very limited Gaelic broadcasting on the radio.

CR

There were several Gaelic associations, such as An Comunn Gàidhealach, Lewis and Harris, Argyll, Caithness and Sutherland – and I did sing for all of them, at their 'cup of tea' ceilidhs. Once a month there was a gathering in the cathedral halls in Albany Street, with a live band involving Neil Morrison and his crowd. It was a full band, with dancing, and songs in between. Robin and I were invited to sing and would get in for nothing because we were performing. Once we were there, Robin would go downstairs to the gents' toilet and open the window to let all our friends in as nobody had any money.

Also, when we first came to the city, Christine and I performed at the local Mod, where we did very well. Then the National Mod was held in Edinburgh in 1960, but by this time a new folk club, the Howff, had opened, and that was my downfall. I wasn't going in for the Gold Medal, because I'm not that type of singer, but I went in for the *puirt-a-beul* competition, in which I came second, with a very high mark in the nineties, but a lad from Laxay, who could never be surpassed, walked it. But as I said, the Howff had opened by that time, and one of the papers reported: 'Tipped winner for this year's gold medal is Dolina Maclennan, who practises by singing Gaelic songs in an Edinburgh beatnik cellar.' Me, a beatnik! That was the beginning of the end of my reputation.

Robin and I performed at the King's Theatre, which the university was given free use of during Charities Week, and I was involved in singing *puirt-a-beul* for a Highland dance group. People started clapping and I had to try and keep the rhythm in my head because the clapping, from different parts of the theatre, was coming to me at different times. The dance society invited me to go to Germany with them one summer, to a festival, which was unheard of in 1959, but I wasn't allowed to go. I had to come home and put up fences and help with the harvest. It was many years later that I actually performed abroad.

Robin's grandfather, Kenneth MacLeod, who was a president of the Educational institute of Scotland, and his grandmother Christina were both from Lewis. Christina was a composer of songs. So there was music from his grandmother's side and Mairi, his mother, was a great musician herself. Every Saturday night at Gray's Hotel, their home in Portobello, she would go to the piano for parlour singing; everything from Ivor Novello to Gaelic songs. Also the D'Oyly Carte Opera Company used to stay there during their whole run at the Lyceum, and on the final night, at the end of their last show, we'd have a party when they would all sing. So I met all those amazing people there.

When Robin and I split up in the early sixties, I stopped singing in the Waverley, but Ian Walker said, "People aren't coming anymore, because it was you they were coming to hear." And I said, "Come on. I don't play the guitar or anything." But he said, "We want you there." So I started singing upstairs in the bar unaccompanied every Wednesday and Saturday, right up until I got married to George Brown in 1963. The Corrie Folk Trio (later The Corries) did their first ever gig in public there one Wednesday night when I was away at Inverurie with Jeannie Robertson. I gave them ten shillings each and showed them how to use the microphone, so they could stand in for me that evening. Roy Williamson always acknowledged that. I remember years later I was playing at the Eden Court Theatre in Inverness and the Corries were performing, and I was coming downstairs and there was Roy, who just gave me a big hug and said, "This is all your fault". I think that was the last time I saw him. I'm still friendly with Bill Smith of the original trio. You never knew who you might be singing to in the Waverley. I remember two extraordinary ladies sitting in a corner, who turned out to be Juliet Greco and Cleo Laine.

The Howff folk club was run by Roy Guest (1934–1996). Oh, the number of people who started out there. It was at 369 High Street, up a flight of stairs. Part of it is now a gallery space. The club was originally opened by a group called the Sporran-Slitters who were some sort of Scottish Nationalist group but I wasn't involved in that. When Roy Guest took it over people like Martha Schlamme, who won fame for her Kurt Weill interpretations, and all sorts of others came to sing there. Bert Jansch started playing there as a fouteen year-old, and he got in everybody's way. The night we had Martha on, the only toilet had broken, so we gave Bert sixpence and a brown carrier bag with string handles to go down to the Mocambo Cafe and get himself a cup of tea and steal their ballcock!

Yes, it was quite a place. We used to make great big pots of soup. Once a man came in and gave someone a fiver to go out and get pies and fish suppers for everybody, which was incredible in those days as you only earned a fiver a week. He said to one subsequently well-known singer, Ray Fisher, "Ye cannae sing lass but you've got a good, raucous voice." Great fun. It was amazing the people who turned up. It was just like the Troubadour in London, where anybody who was anybody in town came. We had Len Partridge, Brownie McGhee, Pete Seeger, Sister Rosetta Tharpe and Davy Graham amongst others.

It was an exciting time and interpersonal relationships could be complex but the music was the most important thing; that and learning from each other. We also stole songs from each other, as when Hamish Henderson, who was careful as to whom he passed the songs he collected, gave Robin Gray and myself *The Plooman Laddies*. We sang it once or twice in the Waverley, but when we went to London to record it for the Topic label we found that Archie and Ray Fisher had recorded it the week before. We were furious. Similarly, when Claddagh Records were making an album of Hamish's own songs he was clear that he wanted Andy Hunter and I to make the first 'authorised' recording of his *Freedom Come All Ye,* under his direction. Hamish was very clear that the words should be sung correctly. To this day I keep saying, to no avail, that there are two things in the song that people often get wrong. It's not '*Will* find breid, barley bree ...', it's '*Can* find breid, barley bree ...' And a line later in the song is often sung as, 'So come all ye...', when it should be, '*Oh*, come all ye ...' The 'Oh' is a plea. Hamish was very adamant about those two words.

☙

In 1963 I married George Brown. George and his crowd used to come in to the Waverley Bar every Friday night before they went on to the dancing at the Plaza or elsewhere, because the pubs used to close at half past nine or ten. He worked for the whisky company MacDonald and Muir, whose brand names were Glenmorangie and Highland Queen, and one of the telegrams at the wedding read, 'Here's to our Highland Queen and her King George.' Our flat became a bit of a base for waifs and strays of the folk scene.

It was George who introduced record producer Joe Boyd to the musicians Robin Williamson and Clive Palmer, who became the core of the Incredible String Band. Boyd had been sent up to

Scotland by Bill Leader and he stayed with us. There's a lovely and humorous account in his book *White Bicycles* of the visit, including his first experiences of Scottish pub life and of meeting Hamish Henderson, whom he describes as, 'a remarkable man ... the last Pictish speaker on the planet'.

Before I got married I went to Glasgow to select my going-away outfit with my cousin, who was to be the bridesmaid. That was a big thing then. When I came back I couldn't get into my flat, so I pounded on the door until a guy came to the door shouting, "Who are you? How dare you. We're recording," to which I said, "Well this happens to be my flat." This was the making of the LP record *Edinburgh Folk Festival* by Bill Leader.

Alex Campbell stayed with us regularly. One night I was singing at the Assembly Rooms and I was just about to begin performing when Alex came in and shouted from the back of the hall, "You've still got the best legs on the folk scene." He was totally incorrigible. It was said that he married a leading American folk singer for £15 so that she could stay in the country. Alex was a dynamic character; a great performer and a great street singer. He could sing kitsch Scottish songs and make them sound cowboyish. Others who stayed included Billy Connolly, Isla St Clair, Cyril Tawney, the Clancys, Aly Bain, Bobby Campbell and Gordon McCulloch who became The Exiles, along with Enoch Kent. Bobby subsequently went to London where he worked in journalism. There was a great bond between many of us that still endures. For instance, years later, Bobby and his triplet sons used to come up and stay with me when I had moved to Perthshire.

The hippies from the Howff used to come in and have a bath and wash their hair and because I was the only one who was working I always had food. One day I had bought two pounds of sausages, which was a big deal. They were in an oval Pyrex dish which was full to the brim with onions and tomatoes and other goodies. Bobby Campbell and Gordon McCulloch were there and some of the other Glasgow folk, and they could smell it through the house. When I shouted, "Ready folks, come and get it," they all rushed into the kitchen, but as I took it out of the oven the dish split in two, and its contents landed all over the red rug which covered the floor.

At another time during that period Dominic Behan was doing a Festival show at the Crown called, 'Behan Being Behan' and he was staying with us. Dominic was very unpredictable and one particular night before he went on, he was quite drunk. George, who could do anything to him without getting punched, put his head under the tap, after which he delivered an impeccable performance. Nobody else would have done that. When we came back upstairs, (the flat had a long, long, lobby with the kitchen at one end and the sitting room at the other), we could hear Liam Clancy singing Dominic's song *The Patriot Game* in the sitting room. Dominic couldn't stand Liam, so this was like a red rag to a bull. I sensed trouble and stood between them saying, "Look, this is my house, there's no fighting here", after which they shook hands and sang it together. Happy days.

There were other kinds of music around then too, such as skiffle. Robin Gray's crowd all played banjos and jazz and I think Bill Smith of the Corries had played with a jazz band as well. It was a more open scene in a way and it was very, very experimental. Then there was the Weavers and *This Land is Your Land*. We sang that sort of thing and others, like *Lassie Wi' the Yellow Coatie* and *Mormond Braes,* but that was all before the big traditional ballads came back in. We didn't know them, although we'd studied some of them as poems at school. We hadn't realised that they were actually ballads, to be sung; things like *Harlaw* and *Tam Lin.* They hadn't been linked back into the folk scene yet.

In 1962 I played in a big end-of-Festival concert, 'Plain Songs and All that Jazz', at Haymarket Ice Rink with George Melly, Caroline Hester, Al Fairweather, the Clancy Brothers, Tommy Makem and others. It was hosted by Rory and Alex McEwen. Rory and Alex were of Border aristocracy, from Marchmont House in Berwickshire. Rory was an abstract sculptor, later becoming a botanical artist of the highest order and I think Alex was a lawyer involved in business. There was a major retrospective of Rory's life and work held at Kew Gardens in 2013. They were regular performers of folk on television and had a show on Border Television; put on possibly because they had local connections. Rory phoned me and asked, would I come and do a spot on Border Television, and would I also be part of their Festival show? I was to be the guest on the Saturday, the last night of the festival.

I'll never forget it, because I had a party at Bristo Place that night, before we all went down to the Waverley. Nadia Cattouse was there, and Sidney Carter, all that crowd. Then a convoy of cars escorted me to Murrayfield Ice Rink. The dress code was black and white and I had gone to Richard Shops on the corner of Princes Street and Hanover Street and bought a short wedding dress in white grosgrain which had pointed cuffs that I cut off. The big jazz band had just come off, and I had to walk out on to that huge stage by myself. I remember Mairi Gray, Robin's mother, saying later, "You looked so lonely. You just came on and I said, 'Oh Poor Doli.' " Then she said, "You sang the *Lament of the MacGregors of Glen Lyon* and you filled the place." She obviously knew how I felt.

Robin Gray and I recorded an extended play record, *By Mormond Braes*, for the Topic label at Bill Leader's house in

London. Eric Winter was the editor of *Melody Maker* then. He had heard us singing at the National Union of Journalists conference at the Assembly Rooms in Edinburgh. He wrote about me all the time and it was he who got us to go down to London. We had to fly from East Fortune because Turnhouse (as Edinburgh Airport used to be called) was closed for upgrading. It was the first time I'd flown and we were seen off by a piper. When I had my tonsils out in 1963, Archie Fisher asked was I going to pickle them and send them to Eric Winter as he had become such a fan! When the disc came out it was the *Woman's Own* record of the month!

In 1963 I sang for the documentary 'Songs of Scotland', made for Films of Scotland by directors Laurence Henson and Edward McConnell. Hamish and I sang *Bonnie Lassie I'll Lie Near Ye* in Scots. It was filmed in the bar of the old Habbie's Howe at Nine Mile Burn at the foot of the Pentlands, with a lively audience joining in the chorus. The documentary took Certificates of Honour at the American Film Festival, New York in 1966 and the American Film Festival, New York in 1969. Hamish Henderson and I also appeared in a film 'Die Armee des Duke' (The Duke's Army) along with singers Jeannie Robertson, Jimmy McBeath, Andy Hunter and the Royal Scottish Country Dance Society, directed by Robert Peter Hertwig and with a commentary by Professor Clemens Kaiser-Breme and another German production, 'Auf Schottischen Schlachtfelden' (On Scottish Battlefields), featuring Jeannie, Jimmy, Andy, Geordie Hamilton, fiddler Simpson Pirie and the Stewart Family. Both were shot in Perthshire and Hamish must have been involved in the consultations for these. Little did I realise that I would be back living in the shadow of Blair Castle some decades later.

☙

Robin and I opened the Howff Club in Dunfermline in 1961, one of the first folk clubs in Scotland after the Edinburgh ones, and I sang at the 'Ledlanet Nights' events in Kinrosshire; a kind of arts festival that operated for around ten years from 1962, at the home of the publisher John Calder. They had opera, theatre, chamber music recitals, orchestral concerts and, quite enlightened for the time, folk music. It was there I remember singing *The Laird o' the Dainty Dounby* in the presence of the Laird of Ledlanet.

Of course, folk music was a close bedfellow of the literary arts back then and I mixed with all the Scottish poets in Edinburgh and toured Ireland once with the poets. I went with Black Angus (Aonghas MacNeacail) and the two Montgomery girls, Catriona and Morag. At that time there was a journalist and broadcaster in Ireland called Seán Mac Réamoinn (1921–2007) who had worked with Seamus Ennis, recording and collecting folklore, and had contributed to the revival of traditional music there. He was very well known, a real character. He followed us around everywhere. One night I was singing *MacCrimmon's Lament* yet again and I took the giggles in the middle of it, because he wasn't there that night; "*Cha till, cha till, cha till Mac Criomain ...*" I also accompanied the Irish poets on their tour of Scotland and, as always, we hosted them in Edinburgh and laid on a party. The Arts Council was always very stingy with the drinks. One Sunday night our house in Thirlstane Road was full of Irish poets and the booze ran out, so I phoned the Police Club. Ian Green, who later founded Greentrax Records, came up with replenishments. He was in the police then. It was an emergency so I just called the police and they dealt with it (don't tell anybody)!

I toured Brittany for a fortnight with fiddler Aonghas Grant and the Stewarts of Blair. I also became president of the Pan Celtic Festival in Killarney in 1983. The main objective of the Festival is

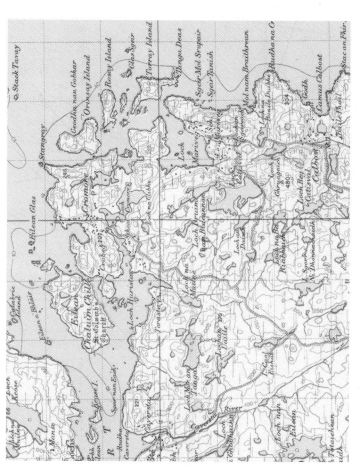

Detail from Ordnance Survey map showing Marvig, South Lochs, 1948.
© National Library of Scotland

Dolina's mother Mary Bell Mackenzie of 13 Marvig

Dolina with Auntie Christina and daughter Mary, 1965

The house where Dolina was born, 18 Marvig

The ruin of Dolina's mother's house

Angus 'Kid' Maclennan in action in Canada

Dolina with her father and Joey the dog at Marvig, 1948

Back Row : John Macleod; 20 Marvig; John A Mackenzie; West End, Calbost; Kenny J Brown; Calbost; Donald A Macleod; 20 Marvig; John Macmillan; 17 Marvig; Calum A Morrison, 9 Calbost.
Second Row :Kenneth A Macleod;3 Marvig; Peggy Macleod;11 Marvig; Muriel Mackenzie, West End Calbost; Sandra Finlayson,10 Calbost; Katie B Macleod,10 Calbost; Louisa Macleod, Calbost; Peggy A Brown, Calbost Mary Macleod, 3 Marvig; Donald R Mackenzie, 7 Marvig.
Front Row: Henrietta Mackinnon,24 Marvig; Mary A Mackenzie, West End, Calbost; Ina Morrison, 9 Calbost; Chrissie A Mackenzie, 12 Marvig; Dolina Maclennan; 18 Marvig; Ann Macleod, 22 Marvig.

SUCCESSIVE NUMBER ON ADMISSION OR RE-ADMISSION OF RE MEMBERSHIP	DATE OF ADMISSION OR RE-ADMISSION			NAME IN FULL CHRISTIAN AND SURNAME	IS ADMITTED ORIGINAL ADMISSION NUMBER	EXACT DATE OF BIRTH			PARENT OR GUARDIAN	
	Year	Month	Day			Year	Month	Day	NAME	ADDRESS
229	43	44	13	Donaldina Maclennan		38	1	1	Angus Maclennan	18 Marvig

Top: Planasker School, Marvig, 1947. Dolina second from right, front row.
Bottom: Extract from Planasker School Admissions register, 1943

Planasker School, Marvig

Planting potatoes with brother Donald

Sister Jessie, sister-in-law Dolina, Dolina's mother and Dolina

The Ebenezer *having its annual re-paint, Marvig*

Dolina's four brothers. From left: Murdo, Duncan, Donald and Murdie John with Neil Macleod on the Ebenezer

SOUTH BEACH AND PIERS FROM GALLOWS HILL, STORNOWAY.

69

Postcard, 'South Beach and Piers from Gallow's Hill, Stornoway'.
Reproduced courtesy of Tasglann nan Eilean Siar.
© Permission sought

Nicholson Institute Girls' Choir with Mr Short at the piano

Nicholson Institute class of Gaelic students with teachers.
Dolina first pupil on right, front row

Postcard, 'South Beach, Stornoway', showing the Louise Carnegie
Hostel in the foreground on the right. Courtesy of Malcolm
Macdonald. © Permission sought

Postcard, 'South Beach Street Stornoway (During Queen's visit, August 1956)'. Reproduced courtesy of Tasglann nan Eilean Siar. © Permission sought

Dolina's first stage play, 'The Dear Departed', Stornoway c. 1955. Dolina seated at table, centre

Portrait of Dolina by T. B. Macaulay, Stornoway, 1955

March past during the Queen's visit to Stornoway, 1956

Dolina with Morven, Woodlands, 1990s

Stuart MacGregor and Bob Blythe, Perthshire, 1958

Dolina with Robin Gray, 1963

Dolina singing in the Waverley Bar, Edinburgh, 1961

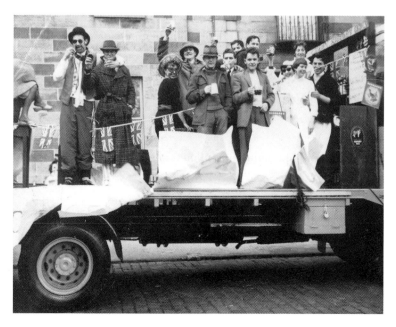

Sandy Bell's float, student charities event, Edinburgh, 1958

Detail from cover of concert programme,
Edinburgh International Festival, 1962

For One Week from
MONDAY, 3rd September 1962
at 10.45 p.m.

THE EDINBURGH FESTIVAL SOCIETY

presents

PLAIN SONG
and all that Jazz

Produced by GERARD FLEVIN

RORY and ALEX. McEWEN

CAROLYN HESTER   **DICK FARINA**

THE AL FAIRWEATHER — SANDY BROWN ALL STARS
and TONY COE

with

GEORGE MELLY

With Star Guests every night

THE CLANCY BROTHERS and TOMMY MAKEM

JULIAN BREAM   LOU KILLEN

DOLINA McLENNAN   SYDNEY CARTER

RED NERK

Extract from concert programme,
Edinburgh International Festival, 1962

Dolina and Morven with Stuart MacGregor, 1958

Norman MacCaig

Dolina and Hamish Henderson about to drive from Edinburgh to Blair Atholl, November 2000

Poster for Heretics performances at Edinburgh Festival Fringe, early 1970s. Note the ticket price!

Sorley Maclean, Dolina and Robert Garioch
while recording the Heretics album

Poster for 'An Clò Mor', Stornoway

Scene from 'An Clò Mor', 1972

The Scottish Arts Council

19 January 1972

Dear Miss Maclennan,

I don't normally write fan letters but I did want to tell you how much I enjoyed your performance in *An Cló Mor* at the Citizens last evening. Both vocally + visually it was superb, and your presence and movement (even in competition with all those dancers) was in the same class. I know what a very heavy responsibility lay on you, and I can only say that you were very moving and gave great pleasure to the whole audience. Congratulations & good luck.

Yours sincerely

Sandy Dunbar

P.S. Don't answer.

19 Charlotte Square, Edinburgh EH2 4DF Tel 031-226 6051 (7 lines) Chairman: Lord Balfour of Burleigh, Director: Alexander Dunbar

Letter from Sandy Dunbar, Scottish Arts Council, 19 January 1972

Press conference, Edinburgh International Festival, early 1980s

Dolina as Mrs Scott in BBC Scotland production of
'Consider the Lilies', c. 2001

*Dolina with Donald Iain Macritchie and Mairi Morrison in
'An Roghainn', by Robbie Fraser*

Flier for proposed Cape Breton Mod, 1985

Watercolour of Woodlands, Blair Atholl

Blue Room, Woodlands

Dining Room, Woodlands

Dolina's friend and neighbour, Donald MacFarlane, Blair Atholl

Bo'ness Rebels Ceilidh, Dolina second left, second row

Portrait of Dolina, early 1970s

to promote and to foster the Celtic languages, music, songs, and games and to urge the interaction of cultures, knowledge and tourism in the countries of Scotland, Wales, Ireland, Cornwall, Brittany and the Isle of Man. Each of the Celtic countries takes it in turn to provide the president for a year. When my year was up, I had a badge of office made by a silversmith who had a place at the top of Candlemaker Row in Edinburgh. I designed it with the emblem, had it put on a silver chain and passed it to the next president. It's still being handed on. I had planned to visit each of the Celtic countries that year when I was president, but circumstances just got in the way, although I did attend the *Oireachtas na Gaeilge*, which is the Irish equivalent of the National Mod, and the Merriman Society's annual event to celebrate Merriman's great poem, 'The Midnight Court'. I represented Scotland at the Eisteddfod as well. The Eisteddfod was broadcast live on BBC2 for a whole afternoon, during which I had to make a speech in Welsh. I did not trust the man who translated it for me and I had to check it with other people because I feared he was a rogue. He was the solicitor who defended the Welsh rebel house-burners; 'Come home to a real fire, come to Wales.'

One time Hamish Henderson brought the pioneering Irish composer Sean O'Riada to visit us. He, Hamish and Ruth, Sean's wife arrived with a bottle of whisky and we really hit it off. He said that when I came to Ireland we were going to do this, that and the next thing and he was going to take me out on his boat, of which he was very proud. I gave him the only recording I had of my family in Lewis singing 'the books'; the Gaelic psalms we sang every night, which George had caught on a reel-to-reel recorder back in 1964. Sean O'Riada had never heard this music before and he was absolutely fascinated, so I gave him the tape. He died very suddenly not long after and several years later, on my first trip to Ireland, when I was there with the poets, we went to an event where they were having an evening to remember him. It was incredible as I was singing *MacCrimmon's Lament*, written for the greatest musician Scotland ever had, in tribute to the greatest musician Ireland ever had. When I finished it was like coming out of a dream as nobody clapped for what seemed like an age before the place erupted. It had never happened to me before nor since and it was just this incredible feeling. Several years later Flora MacNeil and I were at the Pan-Celtic and there was Peadar, Sean's son, playing my family's tape as part of a lecture he was giving. Of course he didn't know the background. He said his father had got it from a Dolina Maclennan and that it was a recording of her family. He didn't realise I was in the audience, and it was very strange hearing my family's fireside psalms in the middle of Ireland.

I was always drawn to the singing of the wonderful traditional Gaelic singer Kitty MacLeod (1914–2000). I was working on a programme for BBC Gaelic and we decided to find her. John Carmichael, who was producing, found her living in Temple, Midlothian, got in touch with her through all sorts of machinations, and asked if I could come and interview her. Over the years she had gone into semi-seclusion, but said yes as she had always been interested in what she'd heard about me and my singing. So one night John came through to Edinburgh and he, George, myself and the girls went down and spent the whole evening with her, recording our conversation. Then she said she'd give me all her songs, but I wasn't to tape them or anything, I was to sit at her feet and learn. But the children were small and I didn't drive at that time, so I never did. I used to go and visit her but I never had the opportunity of getting her songs. She got married again when she was eighty, to a doctor who had been at university with her, and they came and stayed with me in Perthshire on their honeymoon.

She gave me her Iona brooch just two weeks before she died. She said, "The most precious thing I had went to the grave with my sister. I want you to have the next most precious thing." I didn't know it was an Iona brooch, but last year I had it pinned on a cape as I went into the small antique shop in the High Street and the man there said that it was quite rare and that I'd better look after it.

Those folk music reminiscences could carry on for ever, but one last beautiful memory is of a festival in Eindhoven, in the Netherlands. There were lots of us there and on the last night the mayor of the city presented us all with boxes of lovely chocolates. The festivities went on until the sun rose, and as the Glasgow singer Gordeanna McCulloch and I were leaving, the caretaker gave us a big plastic bag full of the remaining chocolates. We were wearing long frocks and proceeded to our hotel, handing out boxes of chocolates to startled early-morning workers, "with the compliments of the Celtic countries." I remember one of them almost falling off his bike.

Chapter 7

With the Poets

I MET poet Norman MacCaig shortly after I fell in with Stuart MacGregor and Hamish Henderson, in 1958. Stuart took me along to Norman's flat the following week. I hadn't heard of him at school, as we had concentrated on historical poets, in both English and Gaelic. He played the fiddle that night, the one and only time I ever heard him do so, despite frequent visits over the years.

Norman could be quite acerbic but I could cope with that, although it took me time to get used to it. I'd go along and he'd say to me, "Sing me one I've never heard," and I'd say, "You've heard them all." "Then sing me one I like," and I'd deliver his favourite, which was "*Toirt m'aghaidh Diura / 's mo chuall ri Port Asgaig*" after which he would command: "Sing it again. Better this time." Sometimes he'd phone at eleven o'clock at night and say, "Are you up lassie?" and he'd come over and we would spend time reading poetry and discussing everyday things. So we had a very special kind of friendship that didn't make demands. He didn't feel he had to show off with me, as he sometimes did in wider company.

There are so many stories about Norman still vivid in my mind. I remember one evening sitting in Leamington Terrace with him on one side of the fire and Christopher Grieve (Hugh MacDiarmid) on the other, and they were flyting as was their wont. Chris was accusing Norman of having never written anything of great merit, and said that, on the other hand, when he himself was gone he would leave a wealth of poetry to the world. He added, "But when you go..." and, quick as a flash, Norman replied, "Ah, but Chris, I'm not going."

There is another wonderful Norman story. It was around 1982 and I was adjudicating at the local Mod in Glasgow. Robin Gray, with whom I'd sung all these years before, was back over from Mexico and came through with me to hear the children singing. It was a beautiful day and when we arrived at Queen Street Station to catch the eleven pm train back to Edinburgh who was standing there but Norman. We all greeted each other. Also waiting on the platform was a folk group that had been playing in Glasgow. As time went on and there was still no train people got restless, so the folk musicians took out their instruments and started playing. The next minute Robin pulled me out and then another couple joined us and then others until we had enough for an eightsome reel on the platform. Passengers and police were standing there, clapping to the music. It was absolutely wonderful, and Norman was saying, "I can't believe this is happening." It was a unique moment, a beautiful little episode that I will always remember. I recently met one of the band members from that night, who also recalls it vividly.

It was I who introduced Aly Bain to Norman. I took Norman along to a party at Aly's and initially they disliked each other intensely, although over the years they became the closest of friends.

The last time I saw Norman was in 1995, the summer before he died, and it was very strange. By that time I was living up in

Perthshire but was back in Edinburgh for the weekend. Finding myself in Bruntsfield, I bought two '99' ice cream cones and, without knowing whether he would be in, walked down towards his house at Leamington Terrace and went up the stairs for what seemed like the thousandth time since I first climbed them in 1958. I heard a shuffle, and he came to the door. "Oh, come in," he whispered. So I gave him a cone and we sat there eating our '99's. It was a poignant final moment together, although I didn't realise that at the time.

It was through Norman that I met Chris Grieve, who could also be very acerbic and cantankerous. We too became great pals and he was a regular guest at our Heretics poetry gatherings. Although it has been said that he could start an argument in an empty house, I vividly remember him sitting between my two daughters' beds, fondly telling them a story. Plenty has been written about the character of MacDiarmid, but my own memory of him is of a gentle, humorous, kind man. However, I do recall that he would never appear on the same stage as the poet Robert Garioch. I have no idea why that was, although Garioch could be quite critical of MacDiarmid. For example, during the Heretics period I was asked to organise a poetry evening for Amnesty International on account of my links to the poets. However, MacDiarmid wouldn't come if Garioch was to be there, and Garioch wouldn't come if MacDiarmid were also to be involved. In the end I think I cancelled both.

The last time I saw Chris was when Isobel, Norman's wife, drove Norman and I to Brownsbank, outside Biggar, which was home to Chris and his wife, Valda. Isobel had a little allotment out there, so Norman and I went to spend a few hours with Chris and Valda while she was tending to her vegetables. We found Chris sitting there, swathed in a tartan rug while Valda was running around looking after him. The flyting between him and Norman went on even then. Chris was quite frail by that time, and I knew it was unlikely that I would see him again. When we were leaving, I said, "Well, goodbye Chris," and he pulled me down and gave me a great smacker of a kiss, chuckled and said, "I always wanted to do that." I treasure a hand-written copy he gave me of his famous poem, 'The Little White Rose of Scotland'.

I also met up regularly with other poetic stalwarts of the day. I don't know where I first met Sidney Goodsir Smith, but it was probably in the Abbotsford bar in Edinburgh's Rose Street. He was an amazing character, and my most vivid memory is of his laughter, which sometimes ended up with an asthmatic attack. He was also a painter and art critic of note and I'm proud to have one of his paintings on my wall. Then there was Robert Garioch, who was famously pawky. He was a lovely but very private person who never gave anything away. Some of his poetry is enormously humorous. The poet I found most difficult to get to know was Tom Scott, although I did meet him later as the person rather than the writer. We used to bump into each other at the Botanic Gardens with our respective prams when he was pushing the twins and I was pushing my daughter Mary, and we always stopped for a blether.

Edwin Morgan used to come through from Glasgow to read for us and he was my introduction to concrete poetry. There was one wonderful free Saturday during the filming of 'The Cheviot, the Stag and the Black, Black Oil' at Dornie, when I climbed to the top of a hill and lay in the sunshine with a picnic and Edwin's latest book of poems. Another memorable occasion was when Norman, Edwin and myself were invited by the Arts Council of Wales to perform in Cardiff. We were in a great auditorium that held three hundred people, but there were less than twenty there because the Arts Council had forgotten to advertise it. We did a token half-hour after which, to their embarrassment, they took us out to dinner. As you can imagine there were some juicy and acerbic comments passed that night.

Of the Gaelic poets, Sorley MacLean was the one I was closest to. I first met him in the Saltire Society rooms at Gladstone's Land in the Lawnmarket, way back in 1958. It was the first time I'd ever heard any poet reading their own work, and he was reading in Gaelic. Sorley had a wonderful sense of humour. I once stayed with him and his wife Renee at Braes on Skye for a few days. One lovely summer's evening, Renee and I were making curtains while Sorley was lying back in his chair, fast asleep, with the paper over his face. Renee said, "I think we've done enough for tonight; we'll just have a wee dram. Himself is sleeping." Then came the voice from under the newspaper, "He's just wakened." Another night, in the George Square Theatre, Edinburgh, one of the many events at which I introduced the poets in public, I announced Sorley before appropriating his seat next to Norman in the front row of the audience. As Sorley fumbled with his books and scripts even more than usual that evening Norman turned to me and whispered, "We knew he was going to read his own poetry, but we thought he was going to read it out loud." As I wrote in The Scotsman, in 1981, when reviewing a 70th birthday exhibition of Sorley's life and work in the National Library of Scotland:

> I think Sorley MacLean's tribute to Hugh MacDiarmid can equally be true of our great Gaelic poet himself – 'Combining a supreme poetic sensibility, an astonishing intellectual energy, with a social and political activism rare in the intellectual.'

I suppose, in retrospect, I felt more comfortable with the poetry of the two major Lewis poets, Derick Thompson and Iain Crichton Smith. The subjects and simplicity of their poetry was more familiar and accessible than the more cerebral preoccupations of Sorley's poetry, which often had to be explained to me. Iain was great fun to be with and I remember him telling me that he had inherited a cottage in Stornoway. Without thinking, I said, "In Battery Park?" And he said "How did you know?" and I said "I didn't. It just came out." I don't know why I said it but I think he was quite wary of me after that!

Derick and his lovely wife, Carol, who was a Mod gold medallist, came to live in Aberfeldy for a while when I was living in Blair Atholl and we enjoyed each other's company and got to know each other better than we had on the poetry scene. He was such an able and self-effacing writer and editor. He sent John Carmichael of the BBC, then a Gaelic student, to interview me for *Gairm*, the magazine he edited for many years. I was also surprised when he included me in his 'Companion to Gaelic Scotland', for my having written the Gaelic radio serial '*Na Moireasdanaich*'.

On many occasions over the years, some of the poets would come back to our flat after a reading for sing-songs, sandwiches, debates and drams. There's a lovely story about Sorley MacLean meeting Norman MacCaig in Bennet's Bar at the King's Theatre, the day after one of those evenings. Apparently Sorley asked Norman, "Did I fall asleep at Doli's last night?" "Not that I noticed," said Norman, to which Sorley replied, "Well, Norman, you see, these days at a certain time of night and after a certain amount of drink, I would fall asleep, supposing I had Helen of Troy on the one side and Voltaire on the other."

Although I was out of my depth when I first met most of them, they all became my friends and, maybe because of my naivety, I never felt over-awed in their company. I didn't go to any of their funerals. I prefer my beautiful last memories of all of them.

Another visitor who became a good friend, especially with my daughter Jane, was Ivor Cutler. He stayed with us because he couldn't stand the muzak in hotels. I have a lovely poem he wrote for us.

෬

The Heretics was formed by Stuart MacGregor with the poet Willie Neill and his wife, Dodo. He had the idea of an informal poetry reading group and it was Dodo who came up with the name. Afterwards she thought it wasn't such a good one, but it stuck. Certainly we were going against the grain, proving a platform for unpublished poets and young musicians, despite the lack of interest and backing from the Scottish Arts Council, who at that time only supported established performers. The idea of the Heretics was to bring poetry and music together in a relaxed pub atmosphere. There was so much creativity around but no opening for it and such a sense of frustration that forming the group was like taking the top off a boiling kettle for many people.

The first Heretics meeting was in May 1970 and we continued for ten years without any support from any arts bodies, because Stuart was such a stimulant in keeping us all going. I wasn't at the original meeting, but my husband George and I joined, along with broadcaster David Campbell, poets and writers Donald Campbell and John Herdman and publisher Gordon Wright. We formed a committee and because our children were young, we used to meet at our house in Morningside Road. Singer Morag Dunbar was also on the committee, and writer Stanley Roger Green. As John Herdman has pointed out, there were some other poetry readings about, such as those run by Alan Jackson and Pete Morgan at the Traverse, but that these tended to feature well-known people like the Liverpool Poets. We had all the major Scottish poets as guests at one time or another over the ten years. It was great to have someone like Willie Neill, who wrote in Scotland's three languages, Gaelic, Scots and English, and Stuart as compere initially. Other people coming and going included Maggie and Liz Cruickshank, Liz Lochhead, Bobby Eaglesham, Adam McNaughtan, Andrew Grieg, Kevin Mitchell, Aly Bain and another two musicians from Shetland, the Smith brothers. Among the poets there was obviously MacDiarmid, MacCaig, Sorley MacLean, Iain Crichton Smith, Edwin Morgan, Derick Thomson, Aonghas MacNeacail, Catriona Montgomery, Willie Neill, Robert Garioch, Tom Leonard, Alex Scott and Tom Scott. Then there was the wonderful Ada Kay (also known as A J Stewart), who believed herself to be an incarnation of King James IV. She looked like Boadicea, with red hair and a long black cloak. And of course we had Billy Connolly around at the time, when he was moving towards being a comedian rather than a banjo-player.

We had the use of a room in the New Town Hotel, and during the Edinburgh Festival we held ceilidhs in the Charlotte Rooms. By the 1980s our meetings had become sporadic, but by that time we'd made an LP record, 'An Evening with the Heretics'. It was recorded for Heritage Records in David Campbell's flat in Dundas Street in 1975.

Gordon Wright had been handling the layout and photographs for the radical nationalist magazine *Catalyst*, which was edited by William Neill before he started his publishing company Reprographia in 1969. His very first issue was a pamphlet of Willie's poem 'Scotland's Castle'. Then in 1970 he published his first major book, 'Four Points of a Saltire', with poems by Stuart MacGregor, George Campbell Hay, Willie Neill and Sorley MacLean. After that he did Donald Campbell's 'Rhymes 'n' Reasons' and

Liz Lochhead's 'Memo for Spring'. They all came out as a result of the Heretics, so we were quite a catalyst.

Apart from our monthly meetings in Edinburgh, the Heretics travelled far and wide, including Glasgow (at the Close Theatre Club, an adjunct to the Citizens Theatre), Greenock, the Buffs Club in Edinburgh, Ochtertyre (where David Campbell did a streak through the sitting room), Wales and Stockton. I don't remember how we ended up in Stockton but it was a disaster and I won't say why!

The Heretics employed the strapline, 'Scotland's Living Tradition' on the heading of a now iconic poster for a Festival season we did in the Charlotte Rooms, Edinburgh. There were three nights: 'Sweetness' with Norman MacCaig and Kevin Mitchell; 'Light' with Billy Connolly, Derick Thomson and Robert Garioch and 'Evil', featuring Hamish Henderson and Aly Bain! The entry fee was fifty-five pence.

Stuart was very dynamic and he loved Scotland with a passion. He, along with Bob Blyth, was the first person to take me to Perthshire, in the spring of 1958. I was working down at Auchen Castle in Dumfriesshire and Bob took us in his old car to Comrie and Killin where we met up with George Clavey, who became a Mod medallist and a well-known Gaelic singer. George had been Stuart's boss when he worked on the hydro-electric schemes, and when he wrote his famous song, *Coshieville*.

> *The west winds blow to Coshieville*
> *And with the winds came we.*
> *But where the river hugs the wood*
> *And blackthorns bloom in May there stood*
> *A single rowan tree.*

So young and tender, so were you,
I loved you both as there you grew
The day I took the road that leads
By Rannoch to the sea.

Stuart also wrote the song *Sandy Bell's Blues* :

Got a little bit too drunk last night,
Broke three ribs in a gutter fight.
How I'm alive I just don't know.
Lay my head down low.
And carry me back to old Bell's bar,
Where all the rogues and the drunkards are.
Only kind of life I know.
Lay my head down low.

And, of course, he gave us *Sandy Bell's Man*:

My father's name's Harry,
My mother's name was Ann.
Come sit down beside me
And dry all my tears.
I've been wronged by a Sandy Bell's man.

He also produced several novels, the best known being 'The Myrtle and the Ivy' and 'The Sinner'.

Stuart left for Jamaica in spring 1972 with his wife, Jane and their children, to lecture in social medicine. Unfortunately, he was killed on Burns night, 25 January, 1973, in a road accident when he was driving from the Blue Mountains. Some years after his death, in 1977, David Campbell and John Herdman scripted 'Stuart MacGregor: A Radio Portrait', which was broadcast on BBC Radio Scotland. This involved poems and songs by MacGregor, as well as a short play written by him and recollections from friends (including myself), colleagues and fellow-Heretics. In this extract, the Narrator (David Campbell), John Herdman and Donald Campbell express their thoughts:

> **John Herdman:** I think the main thing was that Stuart felt that the literary establishment in Scotland was not concerned with the Scottish tradition as he saw it and he felt that writers who did identify themselves with the Scottish tradition in literature and in folk music and so forth were not getting a fair crack of the whip and he started the Heretics really partly as a self-help idea and partly as an idea to give the Scottish tradition more of an airing than it had been getting. Also he wanted to combine the literary aspects with folk music, particularly because he felt that poetry readings were rather dull affairs where people sat on hard benches for three-quarters of an hour. He wanted to bring a livelier atmosphere into it.

> **Donald Campbell:** In many ways, if you read 'The Sinner', the Heretics embodied for Stuart the realisation of a fantasy that had occurred to him in one of his novels. Every reading that Stuart introduced, you felt as if you were about to give a historic reading. He just boosted everybody to a remarkable extent.

> **Narrator:** And it wasn't surprising that Stuart's love of Edinburgh should emerge in his poems at those early Heretics readings.

Reader: 'Northsong'

And if the haar crawls slowly up from Leith
Chilling the flesh and bone, the fang and teeth,
And if the wind turns east in the afternoon
To mock the calendar that points to June,
And if the sky is hard as lead or coal
And streets are tombs that have no sound or soul,
And if the faces of the young and old
Are grey and sad and tired and lost and cold –
I'll wave the sour and moaning heart away,
For in my head I nurse a magic day
When once I walked on Blackford Hill
In sun, after a week of rain and chill;
For at my feet there lay nine shades of green
That kings and southern eyes have never seen.

I always regret that I never took advantage of the opportunity to have my copy of 'Four Points of a Saltire' signed by all four of the poets who feature in the book: Stuart, George Campbell Hay, William Neill and Sorley MacLean. You just don't think of these things at the time.

On the day the news of Stuart's death came, his brother-in-law phoned me, asking me to tell the literati. There was a Neil Gunn event at the Edinburgh University Staff Club that night, so I went there to break the news. John Herdman saw me sneaking in and came to greet me, thinking I had come to join the company (I was touring with Scottish Ballet at the time and had just arrived home that evening). I told John and asked him to tell the assembled company, then left, devastated, as was everybody who had ever known Stuart. It was after that that Norman MacCaig started calling regularly. He had been very friendly with Stuart and I recall him coming in that night and saying, "I'm not crying for him. I'm crying for myself." That expression of Norman's has had a lasting influence on my attitude to friends passing. Stuart had sent me a wonderful letter from Jamaica shortly before he died, talking about the send-off party we had for him and the poems that everyone had written for him, and I regret to this day that I have lost it.

○ঽ

The poet and folklorist Hamish Henderson was another major influence on my life. During the early 1960s Hamish recorded a tape for me to send to the Lewis lads who were in South Georgia for the whaling. Some of the men were away for eighteen months to two years. On it I sang many old Gaelic songs and I remember the boys, when they came home, saying that they really appreciated it and had listened to it all winter long.

Through Hamish I met Ella and Simon Ward whose home was the Edinburgh equivalent of Morris and Marion Blythman's ceilidh house in Glasgow. We would often gather in that house in Bernard Terrace, where I met all sorts of amazing and well known people involved in film and the arts whom you would never expect to bump into, such as the actor-director Sam Wannamaker, who had moved from the United States to England to escape the McCarthyist witch hunt. Simon was retired by then and was a poet in his own right. He always recited the same poem, and he would always finish, "And the grief does not end with the weeping ..." and by this time he'd be crying. I still have a copy of his book, 'Segregated Sonnets'.

The BBC ignored Hamish for most of his lifetime and he had no doubt that he was being deliberately kept off the airwaves.

A high heid yin at the corporation once said to him, "We're out to get you one of these days." He was too anti-establishment; he had communist leanings and was also nationalist, and the BBC wouldn't touch either. When his 'Elegies for the Dead in Cyrenaica' was reprinted, he didn't have a copy of the original first edition, so he borrowed mine, which he'd signed for me. I've only got the second edition now. Hamish didn't care about his appearance, he was terribly unworldly, and sometimes he would go off on a private reverie. He was brought up Episcopalian and, although didn't embrace Christianity as such, he was a very spiritual man. When he retired he wanted to learn Hebrew so he could read the Bible in its original form.

There were great celebrations when Hamish and Kätzel came back from their wedding in Germany, and their home in Melville Terrace was welcoming and hospitable to all. I once spent Christmas with them. It was on Christmas Eve that they exchanged presents, and we had raw herring and beetroot, which was a traditional German dish. The neighbours came in on Christmas Day, and that was another new experience for me, never having really celebrated Christmas at home apart from hanging up our stockings.

Hamish came to stay with me at my guest house at Blair Atholl shortly before he died. I cancelled all the other guests for those ten days he was with me. He was in a big bed in the blue room looking out on the hills. He was in his element. I'd bring him up a cup of tea about half past eight in the morning, and he'd be sitting there reading his favourite from the many interesting books I kept; the story of Evelyn Murray, who was the eighth Duke of Atholl's sister. I remember him saying, "Ah Dolinka [the name he used to call me]. I couldn't ask for anything better than to be lying here in this great big brass bed, gazing at Ben Vrackie and reading my auntie's biography." There were rumours about his origins but I didn't question them. He always had an affinity with the Murrays of Atholl, and indeed with the village of Blair Atholl. His mother had been a nurse at Blair Castle when it was a hospital during the First World War.

By that time he'd gone downhill a bit. I had decided to have a party for him on the Saturday before he left, so each morning he would ask, "Is this my party day?" Martin, the local chef, would take him to the Roundhouse at the Tilt Hotel at five o'clock every night for a nip and a half pint, then bring him home for his tea. That was a very precious time. For the party we invited everybody furth of the Forth, including Jimmy Hutchison, Arthur Watson, Jock Duncan, Pete Shepheard and so many others. It went on from two till seven, and we had tea and scones and beer. It was an amazing afternoon of music and song, and though the place was packed, you could hear a pin drop throughout a ballad that could last for twenty minutes.

Hamish had this total at-home-ness wherever he went. It's well known that he spent a lot of time with the travellers and collected their songs and stories. It was through Hamish that I met Jeannie Robertson, the Stewarts of Blair and many other travelling people.

I still miss them all: Hamish, Stuart, Norman, Sorley and all the rest, and still have one-sided conversations with them.

Chapter 8

Stage

'BEAGAN *Gaidhlig*' was the first ever Gaelic learning series on television, and it was also my first real TV role, as we acted out the parts. There were four of us involved; Evelyn Campbell, Donald John MacLennan, Calum Cameron and myself, and it was directed by George Reid, who would later become the second Presiding Officer in the restored Scottish Parliament. We made twenty-five programmes and through them I became known throughout the Gàidhealtachd and beyond.

As a result of that exposure, I became involved with Scottish Ballet. At that time Stuart Hopps, the company's associate director, had just come to work in Scotland. Stuart had heard Gaelic song in Cecil Sharp House in London and he wanted to do a ballet using Gaelic voice only. He had met George Reid in a pub in Glasgow, a place where all the arts people went, and had discussed the idea with him. He asked if he knew an appropriate singer who could do it, and George suggested me.

The result was '*An Clo Mòr*', 'The Big Cloth'. It was beautifully choreographed. All the dancers had lengths of cloth the same colour as their costumes; browns and greys and blues and greens, the colours of the sea. They swirled the cloths around to evoke a huge storm, and when the waves calmed, a magnificent man came out of them, the survivor of a shipwreck. All the time I was moving among the dancers, singing. I started off with *Calum Sgaire*, followed by various other Gaelic songs. The girls danced around the shipwrecked sailor, singing, "*Caite 'n bidh na maraichean ...*", "Where will the fishermen be, where the seamen will be when the wind is blowing? Dancing with the girls in the white houses of Lerwick."

Then he chose his woman, who was danced by Elaine MacDonald, now Dame Elaine MacDonald, and they did a pas de deux to *Thug-o-ran oro*. I then tied a knot in one of the cloths and put it over them and they did another dance together. It turned out that he was a spectre, he hadn't survived the shipwreck. So he took the cloth from round his neck and put it round hers, and then danced away backwards and vanished, while I sang *Fhir a Bhata*, The Boatman. Morag MacLeod of the School of Scottish Studies helped me choose suitable songs that I already knew, so that I could concentrate on the movement.

'An Clo Mòr' opened in Glasgow's Citizens' Theatre in 1972 and toured Airdrie, Greenock, Beith, Cupar, Dundee and many other places throughout Scotland. On a second tour we went to Orkney and Lewis. It went down tremendously well in the islands. However, there were three dance pieces in the programme, 'An Clo Mòr' being the last one. There was also a piece where the girls were half naked, and there were a few tuts from people who had come to see me, and didn't expect "this kind of thing".

CR

My role in '*An Clo Mòr*' was followed in 1973 by 'The Cheviot, the Stag and the Black, Black Oil'. Bob Tait, who was editor of the magazine *Scottish International*, knew playwright John McGrath, who asked him if he could recommend anyone who could help with Gaelic for a production. By now I'd had quite a bit of exposure through '*Beagan Gaidhlig*', Scottish Ballet, folk singing and the Heretics, so Bob gave him my number and he came to see me.

To begin with I felt quite resentful at the thought of an Englishman coming to tell us about the Clearances, but John phoned, then arrived at the door, saying, "We've come to see Dolina Maclennan." I said, "You must be John McGrath," and he replied, "Yes, is she in?" And I said, "I'm Dolina Maclennan." All the Gaelic speakers that he knew from Sutherland, where his wife Liz's family had property, were quite elderly, so he was expecting me to look about eighty, and here I was in my 30s.

John came in with his wife Elizabeth MacLennan, the actress, and he gave me an outline of the project he had in mind, although it was still very up in the air at that point. By the end of the evening they asked if I'd be interested in joining 7:84 Scotland, which was embryonic at the time (7:84 England had been going for a while before that). John of course had already been writing 'Z Cars' and 'The Bofors Gun' and all manner of other dramas.

The 'Great Northern Welly Boot Show' had just finished and John Bett, Alex Norton and Bill Paterson (who had all been in it, along with Billy Connolly) were recruited right away. The obvious choice for musician was fiddler Allan Ross, who was very experienced in theatre. The famous 'Big Red Book' (a giant pop-up book that formed the set) was designed by John Byrne in conjunction with Allan. All the cast contributed in developing the play.

'The Cheviot, the Stag and the Black, Black Oil' was given its first public reading on 31 March 1973, at a weekend convention, 'What Kind of Scotland?', organised by Bob Tait and *Scottish International* in Edinburgh. George Square Theatre was bursting at the seams with academics and politicians, and we all stood in a row on stage and read what we had handwritten so far. We had had one read through that afternoon before we went on stage with it, but the response that night was unbelievable; there was at least twenty minutes of standing ovation, people shouting and stamping and clapping. It was absolutely overwhelming and we were just looking at each other and laughing and shrugging and smiling. The Sunday papers were full of it.

On the Monday, as we started three weeks of rehearsals, John congratulated everybody then said, "We're really going to start work now. That response will never happen again so forget about it." But it did happen, again and again.

'The Cheviot ...' opened at Aberdeen Arts Centre on 24 April and toured throughout Scotland for almost a year. In a lot of places we were given great hospitality. I think the pivotal thing, which people forget nowadays, was that we managed to enlist the support of the busiest person in the village, and they'd get everybody to come.

The work was tremendously hard as the show was over two hours long, with a short interval, before we changed into the Force Ten Gaels and led a ceilidh, with Liz playing the accordion, Alex playing guitar, Allan the fiddle and, whoever was available was on drums. I'd sing a few songs, unaccompanied, to give them a break, and we'd finish about one o'clock in the morning.

Usually we'd have digs close to where we were playing, but some days we had to drive six or seven hours to get to the next show and set up again. I took cooking stuff with me – food staples and pots and pans – because in those days there wasn't even a chip shop open late north of Inverness, and at the last shop I'd buy mince or a couple of chickens. For rehearsals we were paid £18, while on tour £25 a week. We got paid cash, and every Thursday I took five pounds off everybody and fed the whole cast for the rest of the week. There were only eight of us, with no stage management, so we did everything ourselves. Liz and I did the washing and ironing and one of my other jobs was to unravel the cables for the electrics. We were so poor that we'd use the same gaffer tape over again, rolling it on to a stick and using it again until there was no stickiness left in it.

The reaction to the show was unbelievable. I remember a woman in Harris screaming in Gaelic at John Bett, who was playing Patrick Sellar. I didn't realise at the time that Sellar's son had been the factor for Harris estates, so maybe that was the Sellar she was thinking of rather than the Sutherland one. The Sellars were regarded in the Highlands as worse than the Devil. She just stood up from the audience and put a curse on him. John looked so frightened and turned to me and whispered, "What on earth is she saying?"

Another time (it was in Bettyhill, Sutherland, I think) we were acting out the burning of the writs of eviction when an old man came up and asked us if we realised that the hall was built on the very place where the writs were burned. So we were re-enacting it on the spot where it had actually happened. Murdo MacFarlane, the Gaelic bard in Stornoway, was really shaken by the show, and said he never thought he'd see the history of his people enacted in front of him.

Forty years on, people are still talking about it. It changed the face of theatre and politics in Scotland. Billy Wolfe, SNP leader from 1969 to 1979, had been at the original reading and invited us to perform at the SNP conference in Oban in 1973. John McGrath had said that none of us were nationalists, but I think it was a nationalist play, although in a socialist way. The play couldn't help but be in favour of standing up for your rights. One of our actors came out of character and gave a clenched fist salute to the audience at the end, which didn't go down well. It was as if to say that it wasn't intended for nationalists, it was for socialists.

However, after the next general election there were eleven SNP MPs in Parliament, and I think 'The Cheviot ...' had a lot to do with it, because it stirred people to think for themselves, and also raised consciousness about the land question.

We took it to the Abbey Theatre in Dublin. When we arrived, the Irish press, TV and radio were there and we did excerpts for them. Liz and I were doing the dance of the women of Coigeach, and we wheeched into the wings, where there was an old man doing the curtains who said, "There hasn't been a night like this in here since O'Casey."

Then we toured the west of Ireland. I remember people standing outside at the windows, four to a window, because they couldn't get into one hall in Shannon. Because we were the musicians, Alex, Allan and I were fêted and taken to Doolin, in West Clare, where we spent a whole night playing and singing Gaelic songs. It was great for us to see young people playing music there, learning from their grandfathers. That kind of thing hadn't really started in Scotland.

CR

On another 7:84 tour, 'Boom', there were a couple of lovely incidents. One of the cast, Billy Riddoch, had an accident and ended up in hospital in Golspie, Sutherland. He had to have a general anaesthetic to stitch a badly damaged knee. We were playing Bettyhill and it was sold out, as was usual for there. We couldn't do the show without Billy, who was the principal actor, so we decided that Allan Ross, Alex Norton and I would go there and just do a concert of Gaelic songs and music instead. John McGrath was in Rogart when he heard about the accident, so he went to the hospital in Golspie and insisted that Billy played the part lying on a couch at the side of the stage. In one scene he had to confront some yuppies on motorbikes who were shooting stags, and when he did so one of the actors responded with her usual line which was, "You're not in a very good position to make a statement like that," and both audience and actors fell apart. The following night he did it on crutches.

By the end of the week we were in Oban, where we had two shows, one at nine o'clock in the morning for the school and one in the evening for the public. We had arrived the evening before and Alex took Billy to the hospital to have his stitches removed. The rest of the cast spent the evening re-focussing our lighting rig. After some time, Alex returned by himself and somebody asked, "Where's Billy?" Alex said, "Oh, he's dead," to which someone else replied, "Oh good, no show tomorrow." Quick as a flash, Alex came back with, "But it's all right – I called McGrath and he said he can do it from a coffin at the side of the stage!"

I think it was during the same tour that we were followed by a BBC television crew. One night in Lochmaddy during the post-theatre ceilidh, a fight broke out while I was singing. I didn't stop, even when bodies were falling in front of me. Afterwards the BBC director came up to me and he said, "You would have been great on the Titanic."

Most of the cast of 'The Cheviot ...', including John Bett, Alex Norton, Bill Paterson and myself, became involved in 'The Fantastical Feats of Finn MacCool', by Sean McCarthy, staged in 1974 by the Young Lyceum Company and directed by Kenny Ireland in Haymarket Ice Rink, as part of the Edinburgh International Festival. It told the story of the giant Finn MacCool and there were some lovely pieces in it. I remember the part where the two hounds went after the fawn, played by a beautiful young Irish actress. The actors playing the two dogs followed her up and up, round stairs and through the audience, while I was lying on my tummy right at the top of the theatre, singing a Gaelic song as she changed from a fawn into a woman. Another beautiful scene was when Niamh of the Golden Hair, who was played by Muriel Romanes, took Ossian away to *Tir nan Og*, Land of the Ever Young. Folk singer Hamish Imlach played the giant and the Irish group Planxty sang and played throughout. It was a huge production and took up three weeks of the Festival.

As usual, people regularly came back to our house after performances. I remember on the very last night, Vanessa Redgrave came to stay. I didn't know that she was going to hold a Workers' Revolutionary Party meeting at our place. Alex Norton and I drove to Cardiff the following morning to help write a play called 'The Welsh Knot' for BBC Wales.

ର

Donald Campbell, one of our Heretics poets, had written a play called 'The Jesuit', which dramatised the life and trial of John Ogilvie, the subject of the play. It was produced and toured by the Heretics, and described by Allen Wright, arts editor of *The Scotsman*, as, "one of the most important works to have been written for the Scottish stage in recent times". It was directed by Sandy Neilson, my dear friend Henry Stamper played Bishop Spottiswoode (which was how I met him) and Jimmy Yuill, Roy Hanlon and Martin Black were the soldiers. Beth Neilson played the archbishop's wife and Michael Burrell played the Jesuit himself.

Sandy couldn't come with us all the time so I became the tour manager, doing the wages, seeing to the venues and putting up posters. The first performance was in the Traverse, but when we asked the Scottish Arts Council for a grant, they said they weren't going to fund a tour and this led to ructions. George Brown, David Campbell and myself went to the Arts Council offices at nine o'clock the next morning, with all our literature, crits and tour arrangements in a case and we did a sit-in. Eventually they had a meeting with us and we told them that we'd organised the tour and the press were going to go to town on what was happening, so, on the spot, they conceded. Try doing that with Creative Scotland today!

By sheer coincidence, the play coincided with plans for the canonisation of John Ogilvie. Some people thought that Donald was jumping on the Blessed John Ogilvie bandwagon while in truth it had been written three years before. We had nuns and priests in the audience, and Pastor Jack Glass and his crowd protesting outside.

In those early days, so many of the young actors stayed with George and I. One of them, Martin Black, was involved in 'The Silver Land', by George Byatt, which Chris Parr directed at the Traverse in 1976. George was a lovely man, but he was very into the collective unconscious and this play was very cerebral. I taught the cast a Gaelic waulking song, which they used to sing every time they saw me after that.

There were hardly any Gaelic actors as such until Mairead Ross co-founded Fir Chlis Theatre Company in 1978, although there were a dozen amateur Gaelic dramatic companies. People like John Murray and Dr Finlay MacLeod were writing plays for them, but there was no professional Gaelic theatre.

Later on, in the early eighties, Owen Dudley Edwards wrote a two-hander for me and Sandy Neilson called the 'Eemis Stane', about the work of Hugh MacDiarmid. We performed it in St Cecilia's Hall during the Edinburgh Festival. In it, I had to read the whole of MacDiarmid's poem 'Island Funeral'. Norman MacCaig came up afterwards and I looked up at him for a response, because he was quite forward with his criticisms, as we know, and he said, "You almost made me like 'Island Funeral'." That was praise indeed.

Fir Chlis Theatre Company was based in Harris and after some memorable performances, it folded, probably due to the remoteness and the heavy costs of touring. It certainly wasn't for lack of ability and talent. The next Gaelic theatre company to start up was Tosg and I did several plays with them, my favourite of all time being '*An Treas Fad*', 'The Third Peat', written by John Murray and directed by Simon Mackenzie. It was the most beautiful thing I've ever done. It was a true story about a widow on Lewis in the early 19th century and her two sons. I wept every night on stage when the recruiters took my youngest son away, and he turned round and said, "Oh Mother, would you sell me for a little bit of land?" It was a hard thing to deal with, even in a play. The younger son was played by Davy Walker, who still calls me "Mammy". I also played his mammy in the Gaelic TV series '*PC Alasdair Stiùbhart*'.

Another memorable Tosg play was '*A Chuirt*', 'The Court', by Ian Crichton Smith, written before his related short story, 'Consider the Lilies'. It was the story of the deceased Mrs Scott, bearing witness at the trial of the infamous factor, Patrick Sellar, who had burned her cottage down. I played Mrs Scott, who returns as a ghost to give evidence at the trial. It was a wonderful piece and was the last stage play I did directed by my great friend, the late Simon Mackenzie.

During the 1980s, Catherine Robins, who was director at the Eden Court Theatre in Inverness, got in touch with me about a production called 'The Crofting Act', which was to mark the 1986 centenary of the act. Catherine had invited eight writers to devise eight separate scripts about different aspects of Highland and crofting life. The contributors were Caroline Proctor, Donald Campbell, Domhnall Ruadh, George Gunn, Catriona Montgomery and Norman Malcolm MacDonald. James Shaw Grant, author, editor of the *Stornoway Gazette* and a chairman of the Crofters' Commission, gave us lots of advice while Capercaillie, who were just getting underway at the time, provided the music. It was an enjoyable but hard-working tour, taking in the highlands and islands as well as Glasgow and Dumfries and Galloway.

I recall that one memorable scene involved the ferry crossing the Minch and passing the Russian klondykers anchored in Loch Broom. They greeted each other by waving and shouting the only word they could share: "Maradona!" Another hilarious scene involved a girl who had been working on an estate on one of the islands where the landlord had a penchant for seducing the lassies who came to work there for the summer.

My next Eden Court play was 'The Wedding Party', Iain Crichton Smith's free adaptation of Bertolt Brecht's 'A Respectable Wedding'. I played the bride's mother and Roy Hanlon played the father. Iain came in a couple of times during rehearsals to execute changes in the script and on one occasion was musing as to how he could find the time during his busy week. He was busy with other things on Thursday, Friday, Saturday, and somebody piped up, "And on Sunday you'll be reviewing the Bible." "No," said Iain, "I'm waiting for a signed copy."

Catherine Robins, whom I've mentioned, had also originated Theatre Workshop in Edinburgh, way back in the sixties. Decades later, I was invited by the then director, Robert Rae, to take part in 'The Hogmanay Boys'. It was set in South Uist, featured Alyth McCormack as the singer, and it was my first experience of working with disabled actors. Again, I taught them Gaelic songs. It was a very physical show and I was amazed at the rough and tumble involved, despite my fellow cast members being in wheelchairs, and at the humour they brought to bear on life in general. In all my years in theatre I have never heard so little moaning and groaning among the cast.

I did several plays with Theatre Workshop, finishing up with Beckett's 'Endgame'. Henry Stamper used to coach me over the phone; "No! Don't say it like *that*, Doli, say it like *this*!" I'm not sure if I ever really understood the play, or if I ever will.

Why do we do it, especially touring theatre? People ask, "What's your real job?" but few appreciate the stresses of not knowing where you're going to lay your head, vans breaking down or ferries not sailing. You don't know whether people are going to come out to see you or not. If there's a death in the village, for example, or a communion weekend, or a local wedding even, having booked months ahead you might arrive, set up and have only three people turn up.

That happened in Ness, on Lewis, with 'The Cheviot ...'. When we arrived at the hall, we heard that there had been a death in the village and, for the first and only time, we had to cancel. Rumour has got round over the years that the local minister had forbidden people to come, but I want to make it clear that that was not the case.

Having said all that, there is nothing more fulfilling than playing to an appreciative audience, whether it's a main theatre or a village hall. I suppose roaming is in my genes.

Chapter 9

Writing and Broadcasting

THANKS to the solid and broad education we received on the island, writing essays and descriptive compositions came naturally to me, but it wasn't until the 1970s that I did any professional writing, when Jo MacDonald, a BBC schools radio producer, asked me to translate the stories of Romulus and Remus and Orpheus and Eurydice into Gaelic for schools broadcasting.

I also did a lot of writing for schools religious programmes, in English, now archived on CD. I'd be engaged to write on a theme – the first one was based around the rune of hospitality and the old line, "I saw a stranger yestreen ..." They were commissioned by David Campbell, who was a BBC producer back then.

Then I wrote one about family feud, which is usually over land or money, but I decided to write it about a dispute over a pipe tune. Shortly after that I wrote a serial for children called 'An Dola', 'The Doll', which came out every Saturday for eight or ten episodes. I've lost the script but I'd love to publish it. Following that I got a commission to write a series of ghost stories. I still tell them as tales and people believe them, so that's all right. They were all broadcast on BBC Radio nan Gaidheal.

I suppose my biggest challenge and achievement was writing '*Na Moireasdanaich*', 'The Morrisons', which became a milestone in Gaelic broadcasting. It was in 1976 and I was in bed with 'flu and the radio was on. I was listening to the news and 'The Archers' followed and as I listened a voice said inside my head, "Why doesn't someone write something like this nearer home?" And another replied, "Why don't you?"

It started from there, and when I felt better I got in touch with Fred MacAulay, head of Gaelic BBC, and I told him I had this idea for a Gaelic soap. He said that somebody else had had the same idea and that he'd asked for six episodes: "I got one good one, one bad one, and I'm still waiting for the rest." I said, "Well, that wasn't me and it was a long time ago," and we agreed to meet. It was the first and only time that I was in Edinburgh's Oxford Bar when the proprietor, the irascible Willie Ross, was there, but we had to leave before lunchtime before his regular clientele came in, because I was a woman. We had a coffee there and went on to lunch and discussed my idea. At that time there were three Gaelic producers' jobs going in the BBC. I applied for one of them and I had great hopes of getting it, because it would have been a permanent position, and I knew a little bit about media by that time.

Eventually Fred phoned and I asked him, "Have I got the job?" He replied, "What job?" "The producer's job," I said, and he replied, "Don't be silly. Your place is not behind the scenes. I want you to write twenty-four episodes." I nearly fainted; twenty four episodes and I hadn't thought in terms of more than half a dozen. But I did it – in twenty-four weeks. It was about an island family, the Morrisons; mother, father, son leaving school, older brother on the oil rigs and a daughter nursing in Glasgow. The neighbours also had central roles. One of them, my own character, Seonaid Kate, was the funniest. She had worked away, in the 'big hoose', and her Gaelic was peppered with English. She would say things like, "*Tha mi* speechless!" She thought she knew everything about everybody. I based her on two characters in my own village, but I won't tell you who.

One of the old neighbours was played by James Mackenzie. In the series, everybody knew he made up stories about himself, saying that he had been all over the world and had won medals in the war, when in fact he had never left the island. I remember writing one chapter in which the Morrisons' younger son collected him to take him to a party, and that's when the denouement came. He started describing how all the ornaments and lamps and things in the house had actually been brought back from America by his sister, who had sailed on the *Metagama*, a famous emigration ship to Canada during the 1920s. Then he said, "But they wouldn't let *me* go at all," admitting it, but only to the young lad, because when they get to the party, he starts being his old self again, with his usual outrageous yarns. But we know that underneath this blustery nonsense, he's quite self-aware. He was my favourite character.

So I wrote twenty-four of them and when the last one was broadcast, Fred congratulated me, saying it was the first time it had been done and it had all come from my own imagination, with no help from any other writers – and, he added, I had just promised to write another twenty-four! That was the first I'd heard of it, but I did it. In total I wrote fifty four – two lots of twenty-four, then he asked me to write another lot, but I only managed six. By that time I was absolutely dry. I left the story open by sending the characters to New Zealand to visit relatives. I didn't kill them off.

Peculiar things happened during the writing of '*Na Moireasdanaich*'. I wrote one about a drunk-driving episode in which someone was killed, and shortly afterwards, someone died in the same place that I was visualising, which frightened me. Also, I had been to Ireland and had discovered community co-ops or *co-chomunns*. At that time, 1976, they hadn't started in Scotland, so I decided to introduce a community market garden, using polytunnels, to the story.

John Angus MacKay had played the older brother who was on the oil rigs, so I called John Carmichael, the producer and asked him to get in touch with John Angus and see would he be available for most of the next series, because I wanted him to be in charge of this *co-chomunn*. So John called me back and asked, "What was it you were going to have him do?" and I explained and he said, "Well you'll never believe it but he's just gone to the Highlands and Islands Development Board to develop *co-chomunns* in the islands." Wow!

I went on from writing for radio to writing for theatre and created a play for Eden Court, 'Search for the Seasons', explaining the folklore of the passing year for children. Simon Mackenzie and I went round schools, doing autumn and winter first. At that time there was a project, 'Growing up with Trees', in Perthshire, so I got thirty-two saplings of hazel and rowan, which were planted at all thirty-two schools involved. We explained about the magic of the rowan and the wisdom of the hazelnut. In olden days the milk of the hazelnut was put on a baby's tongue when it was born, to ensure wisdom. We toured this in the autumn, then went round the same schools again in the spring with the spring and summer parts of it.

When we got to the schools they had whole corridor walls lined with paintings that they had done about the seasons and the trees we had planted. Possibly every school in the highlands now has a rowan and a hazel tree.

The last thing I wrote was '*Isean deireadh linn*', 'The Last Little Fish in the Net'. That's what the last member of a family is called, especially if you're years after the rest. It was based on an unpublished George Mackay Brown essay, 'How the Sabistons Came to Orkney', about how a woman and her mother lived in a thatched cottage near the shore. One night during a terrible storm there's a slap at the door and they think it is a seal but it's a shipwrecked Spaniard. They nurse him and eventually he and the daughter get married. She can't pronounce Sebastian so she says "Sabiston". I combined it with the story of the Gaberlunzie Man – King James V of Scotland was supposed to have roamed his kingdom disguised as a beggar, or gaberlunzie man – but in my version the king goes round visiting all his daughters in disguise and only Isean gives him hospitality. The rest throw him out, thinking he is a beggar.

My story was pulled to bits by the director and cast, so that by the end it wasn't really my play at all, although it was still voted the best children's play that Christmas by BBC Radio Scotland. However, the experience put me off writing and I haven't been able to write any drama since.

I've also written bits and pieces of verse over the years, but have still never considered myself a poet. I wrote the poem below about John Maclean in 1979 after I had seen Freddy Anderson's play about him, 'Krassivy', which won a Fringe First. This coincided with a dinner marking MacLean's centenary in Glasgow City Chambers, at which the poem was read. It was subsequently published in the magazine *Crann-Tara*.

'For John Maclean'

At last, a first for you Maclean
On your hundredth birthday
On the fringe,
Where they always tried to keep you;
But tonight you are the focal point
Chains are glittering for you
But not the kind of chains you were used to,
And we are force-feeding ourselves in your honour.

☙

During this time, I was also broadcasting on radio. My first radio job came shortly after 'The Cheviot ...', when producer Mike Shaw of BBC Radio Scotland asked me to present '12 Noon' on Mondays and Fridays. I'd done the Gaelic learning programme, *'Beagan Gaidhlig'*, on television, but this was radio and it was live, and I hadn't done any presenting.

I got to interview some very interesting people, including Donald Caskie, the wartime minister known as the Tartan Pimpernel, and Lavinia Derwent, who wrote much Children's Hour material including 'Tammie Troot'. I went on to present Gaelic radio and television programmes and at one time my life seemed to be centred round Queen Street in Edinburgh and Queen Margaret Drive in Glasgow, both of which had wonderful atmosphere which is sadly lost in both the new buildings which have replaced them.

After *'Beagan Gaidhlig'*, my next major television job was presenting 'Growing Points'; the 'God Spot', along with Colm Brogan and Jimmy Black. This was on BBC TV every Sunday and, as I said in an interview in the *Radio Times* in April 1977, "It was only when I left Lewis that I began to realise there were ways of expressing faith outside the Free Church – and indeed outside any church. I like the idea of raising the tolerance threshold."

I didn't get a dress allowance, so what I did was get in touch with people involved in craft work. I got a couple of jerseys from Ian Noble's knitting mill in Skye, hand-knitted jerseys from Shetland and one of my sister-in-law's knitted jumpers from Lewis. I wanted this to promote Scottish crafts.

In one of the programmes I interviewed the then Moderator of the Free Church, Professor Cameron, and of course they don't watch television at home on a Sunday, at least they didn't then. My sister told my mother that Dolina was on television last night. "Oh yes, on the Sabbath?" "She was interviewing the Moderator, Professor Cameron," my sister said. To which my mother replied: "What would the Moderator be doing speaking to a clown like her?"

We also had people like Aly Bain and Hamish Henderson on, who didn't necessarily have any established faith. It wasn't a preachy programme, but was about the different ways in which you can show spirituality without necessarily being part of an organised religion.

ᘏ

In 1990 I became involved in '*Machair*', STV's Gaelic soap, which ran for seven years. I played Ishbel McIver; "Ishbel the fairy", as one of the other cast members, Anne Swan, used to call her. Ishbel was a wonderful character. I didn't realise how much she had become part of my life until the series finished.

It was all filmed on location until the studio was built in Stornoway. We used houses all over Lewis, and Ishbel's house was in Grimshader. It turned out to be the family home of my oldest friend, Christine Fletcher. It was her granny's house and I'd been there for weekends when I was at school, which was really strange. I really missed '*Machair*' when it ended, although it's still shown regularly on BBC Alba. I find I can't watch it any more since Simon Mackenzie and Ishbel MacAskill are both gone.

Then I did Findlay J Macdonald's autobiographical series for BBC Scotland, '*Gruth is Uachdar*', 'Crowdie and Cream', set in Harris during the thirties and forties. Findlay and I had worked together on radio a lot; and he was a lovely man. The series was filmed in Harris and we were able to spend the whole summer there, rather than coming and going. I played the part of Findlay's aunt. The Lewis accent is very different from the Harris one, but I was very fortunate in that my friend in Blair Atholl, Chrissie Crichton, came from Leverburgh. We say, "*Mi heeen*," but they say, "*Me henn*," so Chrissie taught me to say it all in a Harris accent. Director Bill MacLeod was a native Gaelic speaker, so that helped a lot. It was a glorious, hot summer and it was a pleasure being part of that six-hour-long production.

Later, during the filming of the TV drama '2,000 Acres of Sky', starring Michelle Collins, I found myself in Galloway for the first time. I was only in one episode, but, since it was done on location, I was contracted for eight weeks.

Of course, I was combining the filming of this and '*Machair*' with running my guest house in Blair Atholl, so life was hectic. On one occasion, while travelling down from Perthshire, I got picked up for speeding, much to the hilarity of the cast, who relished the thought of granny doing the ton.

I also wrote and presented a TV documentary for Pelicula Films called *'Cogadh is Ceol'*, 'The Gael in War', which was shown on BBC 2. There was a programme on the cattle drovers on television one night, quite late, and I had previously done a documentary with Mary Sandeman, telling the story of them and the songs. The programme I saw was dreadful, so I had the idea of doing *'Cogadh is Ceol'*, about the Gael in war with the pipe tunes, the songs and the poetry that came out of it. I phoned Douglas Eadie, the producer, who claims it was two o'clock in the morning when I called, but it gets an hour later every time he tells the story. If you don't act on those ideas when you get them they never happen. He thought I was off my head. "Who'd want to do a thing about the war, glorifying war?" But a few days later he phoned back and said, "I've been thinking about this ..."

We went as far back as 1644, the Battle of Inverlochy, and went right up to interviewing veterans from the last war. Allan MacDonald played all the pipe tunes, Margaret Stewart and Donnie Murdo MacLeod sang and Simon Mackenzie and Chrissie Bannerman read the poems. Peadar O'Riada, the composer and musician, came over from Ireland to contribute to it.

Some time later my agent phoned me and said that Stephen Frears wanted to meet me, to which I said, "Who's Stephen Frears?" because I'd never heard of him. And she said, "Stephen Frears, the director." He was coming up to the Edinburgh Festival and she said she'd be back in touch to tell me when. It was a Sunday morning and he wanted to see me at the Sheraton hotel, opposite the Usher Hall. There was a huge crowd there. I told reception I was there to see Mr Frears, and as I was crossing over to take a seat, a man came in with a huge load of newspapers. He looked at me and said, "Are you the one I'm looking for?" I said, "If you're Mr Frears, yes."

That led to a part in 'The Queen'. We just sat and chatted, and later someone said to me, "Have you got it?" I said that I wouldn't hear for weeks. That was on the Sunday and on the Tuesday my agent phoned and said, "He doesn't want to see anybody else." So I had the part of the telephonist at Balmoral. I didn't meet Helen Mirren. That day there was just myself, the man who played the Queen's equerry and his secretary; just the three of us actors on the set, in a castle near Inverurie, because of course we couldn't use Balmoral.

I was there for just two days and we stayed in Aberdeen airport hotel. It was quite a change after working on a shoestring to suddenly find you're one of just three actors there with eighty crew. Everybody had three assistants and so on. But it was very enjoyable. Stephen Frears doesn't really direct you; he leaves you to do it as you feel like doing it. I asked him, "But why me?" and he told me it was because he wanted someone who sounded like that woman in 'Whisky Galore'.

I have taken part in countless TV and radio programmes throughout the years, and as time goes on it is good to see so many young people; highly trained actors, writers, producers, directors, camera and sound operators, speaking Gaelic on set.

Chapter 10

An Comunn Gàidhealach

APART from attending the Saturday night ceilidhs in the English Speaking Union or in church halls in Edinburgh, I had very little to do with An Comunn Gàidhealach, until one night during the early eighties when Morag MacLeod of the School of Scottish Studies insisted I came to a meeting of the Edinburgh branch. I had no idea why she was so insistent but by the end of the evening I knew, because I was elected branch president. They had obviously talked about it beforehand.

So I took it on, not knowing what was involved. I didn't realise then that there were about five committees within the organisation which as a branch president you were elected on to, and that was quite a problem for me. At that time the Edinburgh branch didn't have more than about twenty members and no money at all, so at my first meeting I said that we would hold a big concert. Of course everyone said, "Oh, we can't do that because we haven't got any money." I went ahead and managed to get the hire of George Square Theatre for nothing and I asked all the performers I knew, including Flora MacNeil and the Boys of the Lough. It was well advertised and the place was packed. Pipe Major George Stoddart and three other members of the Eagle

Pipers' Society played down through the aisles on to the stage and played an opening set. At the end of the night we had we had about two hundred new members and £400 in the bank.

But it all ran away from me. Once they heard at HQ in Inverness that I'd been successful with the Edinburgh branch, they started taking an interest. I can't remember how many committees I had to attend; sometimes they were in Oban, sometimes in Inverness. I was bothered by it, because I didn't see the need for all those meetings. Also I found that having worked with 7:84, where we operated as a democracy, all the decisions with An Comunn Gàidhealach were made in advance of the meetings; such as who was going to be voted for and who wasn't and who was going to say what. I found that very disturbing, but being new to it I couldn't say anything. That opened my eyes to a lot of petty politics within organisations.

Calum MacLeod, who'd been running the National Mod for decades, was due to retire, so I was asked to apply for the job, and I got it, for a salary of about £7,000 a year. I accepted the offer, but it may have been a terrible mistake, because it coincided with a low period in my personal life. However there two things that I'm really proud of from my time with the organisation: firstly, I managed to raise the status of the traditional singing competition, which at that time was not highly thought of nor cared about. The Gold Medal was the big one but the Traditional Competition was much less formal; you sang songs of your own choice, instead of the prescribed songs which were written down, to be followed note perfectly. In traditional song you just sing. It's like the difference between tackety boots dancing and doing the Circassian Circles on tippy-toes. As I was also involved with the Pan-Celtic Festival in Killarney it was arranged, with the encouragement of Fred MacAulay, that the winners of both the male and female traditional competitions would automatically also compete in the Irish festival. The traditional song prizes suddenly became much more attractive and prestigious.

The situation was summed up by the late Fred Macaulay in an article on Gaelic folk song he wrote for the magazine *Chapbook* (Vol. 3, No. 4):

> The greatest criticism one can level at An Comunn is that it imposed on Gaelic music the same pattern as that found in neighbouring cultures, not realising that perhaps it might not be particularly suitable. The piano scale and four-part harmony might conceivably be all right for some songs, but for the large number in the pentatonic and septatonic scales, with their flattened notes, there was no place. In a short time, however, many of them were made to conform, in the process losing character and individuality; but luckily in spite of the published versions, traditional versions still survived, and even today we can make direct comparisons.

ନ୍ଦ

Secondly, I organised a grass-roots reaction to the 1981 private members' bill on Gaelic promoted by the late Donald Stewart, SNP MP. Among other things, it would have given official recognition to the language, obliged education authorities to provide Gaelic teaching in Gaelic-speaking areas and authorised its use in legal proceedings. As the bill was going through Parliament it was filibusted, so I organised a march along Princes Street, called '*Cothrom na Feinne*', 'The Power of the People'. It was led by Ruairidh Mackay and all the big men of An Comunn, along with the Vale of Atholl Pipe Band. There was a huge turnout and whilst I'm not sure what good it did, I know it showed at least that we weren't prepared to just sit down and accept Westminster's attitude to our language.

At the time I also wrote to every MP in Scotland (of course we didn't have a Scottish Parliament then) and all those letters and their replies are now archived in the National Library of Scotland, for the public record. During that time I received a letter from the Mayor of Sydney, on Cape Breton Island in Nova Scotia, suggesting we take the National Mod there. Two of us flew over to talk about arrangements. They were even planning to extend the local runway to receive all the anticipated flights from Scotland, but what An Comunn Gàidhealach committee members were more worried about was how to insure the trophies for travel. I didn't give a toss whether we took the trophies across with us or not; the main thing was to promote our language and culture and to support our Gaelic diaspora in the New World.

To that effect, I'm afraid I caused a little bit of a stir at a meeting in Antigonish. We were making speeches about why the Mod was coming to Nova Scotia and why it was important. The front few seats were taken up by all those important gentlemen in kilts. I suggested that the Mod was nothing at all to do with chieftains or landowners, but everything to do with the language and its continuance. I added that it was because of the behaviour of Scottish clan chiefs in the past that most of them were there, as exiles. Well, this led to a mass exit from those at the front, but at the back of the hall everybody started clapping, illustrating a division of opinion that still exists. So, of course, there was a complaint made against me.

I was *feisaire*, director of the Mod in Perth, Skye, Fort William and Motherwell. When I compered in Perth I conducted it in Gaelic, and there were complaints about that too because people didn't understand what I was saying. But why, I asked, in An Comunn Gàidhealach, should you have to apologise for speaking your own language?

There were four officers employed by An Comunn at that time, including Donnie MacLean, Colin Spencer and myself. We three were quite radical, but the organisation got rid of all of us, one after the other, by fair means or foul. I had the presence of mind to resign, Colin took them to court and they took Donnie MacLean to court. They just did not want change. We wanted to modernise the Mod, get rid of so many archaic things and try to spruce it up. In the first Mod that I ran, I had a Gaelic disco for the children. Change has to come. There are still some competitions with dozens of little children under twelve, all reciting the same poem. Surely there's room for a more imaginative approach?

It wasn't a happy time at all because my personal life was falling apart and I didn't like what I was doing or the whole set up, however there were some memorable times. I had lunch with the Queen in Glasgow City Chambers, but made the great mistake of asking two or three of the ladies on the committee to help me choose a dress, something I would normally do with friends. I just didn't realise the claws they had and that they were absolutely furious that I'd been invited. It was all so small minded. I'd been in the school hostel from the age of twelve, then at the occupational therapy hostel, I'd worked with folk musicians and then 7:84, always within a group, and I never met such pettiness as I came across in An Comunn Gàidhealach.

That's all I really wish to say about it. I met a lot of really wonderful people, especially the late Ruairidh Mackay, who was a giant among men. Ruairidh was a lawyer in Inverness and a historian who knew everything about the country. His Gaelic, which he learned at Fort Augustus School, was immaculate. Travelling with him was a memorable experience because he had a story for every place that you passed through.

I came into An Comunn as a breath of fresh air to some but a cauld blast to others. I was full of enthusiasm and energy and youth, but it didn't work and I view it now as a sad interlude on my journey.

Chapter 11

Memoirs of a Bag Lady

A BOUT the early eighties, my journey seemed to have reached a crossroads with no signpost. My marriage of eighteen years was breaking up, my health was deteriorating, my girls were of an age when they didn't need me and I was so very unhappy in my work. Of course, as I learned when I fell off my bike back in 1953, it was all my own fault ... and, of course, it is a sign of weakness to seek help!

My health began to suffer. I began to have very severe asthma attacks, and was frequently taken to hospital with sirens blaring. This went on until the early nineties, when I underwent a course of homeopathy and the asthma eased. I also lost my sense of smell and it still hasn't come back, nearly forty years on.

During the 1990s I was diagnosed with the inflammatory bowel condition Crohn's Disease. Now, this was very debilitating, with constant 'runs', bleeding, weight loss, depression and a lack of bowel control. For over five years it was constant, day and night, resulting in blood transfusions and continuous steroid treatment. All the money I made was spent on Chinese medicine, herbal remedies, hypnotherapy and the like. However, I did manage, somehow, to keep working, though on one theatre tour 'Doli's bucket' became an essential part of the props! It would have been very easy to become an invalid, but in spite of my stoicism there were some truly awful moments such as 'accidents' in a hotel lift, in John Lewis, Safeway and in the car, that now seem like nightmares. I came to know the location of every loo in Scotland but one good thing was that I suffered little or no pain.

In February 2003, after a highly enjoyable Christmas season with 'The Hogmanay Boys' at Edinburgh Theatre Workshop, I returned to the city for the weekend to visit friends and see a play. On the Saturday morning I suddenly had acute abdominal discomfort, with the need to make 'visits' every fifteen minutes or so. This continued and by Monday morning I was incapable of driving home to Perthshire, heading instead to the accident and emergency department of the Western General Hospital. There I was tested and treated for three weeks before being told eventually that my colon was in very poor order. I did not have Crohn's Disease after all, but ulcerative colitis, which required that I have my bowel removed immediately.

And so it was. The morphine helped but the realisation of what had happened to my body so quickly was traumatic. I coped quite well with my new stoma and bag (known as 'little Willie' and 'the sporran') but took several months to recover my strength and energy, not to mention my weight, which at one point had dropped to six stone. I had a lazy early summer but then managed to film three half-hour documentaries, '*Cogah is Ceol*', with Pelicula Films for the BBC, finishing in September.

Back in April my Edinburgh surgeon had said that since I did not have Crohn's or cancer and was free of disease I was suitable for an ileo-pouch, so in October we went for it. 'It' was a pouch made up of sections of the small intestine sewn together like a miniature rugby ball and attached to the rectum thus removing the need for the stoma and bag. The operation was successful and I was home ten days later, tired but fine. However, one week later it was discovered through a routine blood test that my potassium level was dangerously high and so I was sent to Perth Royal Infirmary. There I was treated for four days, but came home on heavy antibiotics on account of two areas of cellulitis where the intravenous drips had been located. Another week on and I was back at the Infirmary with palpitations, due this time to wrong sodium levels and this saw me attached to the drip once more. Although I had almost reached my fighting weight of eight stone I began to disappear again and I had further tests. These revealed that I had the bug Clostridium Difficile and so I was immediately moved to an isolation room, where I was deprived of all hugs, handshakes and other contact, visitors having to disinfect their hands before leaving.

After two weeks in Perth Royal Infirmary I was moved to the infectious diseases ward at Ninewells, Dundee. A month on the intravenous drip resulted in all my veins hardening to the degree that my arms were covered in kaolin poultices and they had to resort to taking my blood pressure from my ankles. It was like solitary confinement. There was no ward, only individual rooms sealed off from the corridor and I would just see nurses at medicine and mealtimes. I would get through the day reading, doing crosswords, listening to the radio and watching the car park, a couple of trees and some striking sunsets. I had a television but never watched it once. It would have been an intrusion. I had the most wonderful treatment in Dundee but missed the visitors who came when I was at Perth and Edinburgh. I was also fed huge white bread sandwiches – at that time they were unaware that they were killing me.

After I was discharged from Ninewells things did not really improve. I was still producing abnormal quantities in my poor wee bag and could never be far away from a toilet, although it was not as dramatic as before. I was taking large doses of Imodium and the like but nothing helped. I continued to lose weight and by mid-February I was barely able to walk and feeling ready to give up, weighing under six stone. My daughter, Jane Bechtel, took me to the local hospital where the duty doctor took one look at me and arranged for me to be admitted to Edinburgh Western General. After a couple of days I had stabilised and more tests began, under the supervision of the wonderful Professor Dunlop.

Shortly afterwards I was advised that I was found to be Coeliac. That meant no more oats, wheat, barley or rye but I was so happy I could have turned cartwheels and, despite my new regime, I celebrated by eating the packet of jaffa cakes I had just bought before embarking on my gluten free diet for life. Within twenty-four hours my system was improving and a few days later, armed with packets of gluten-free goodies and a positive attitude, I was discharged.

The question remained: why was I never tested for this condition in the twenty years I had suffered? I remember distinctly telling the consultant in Perth years earlier that my sister had this condition but no, over the years I was fed enough steroids for symptomatic relief to ban a whole cycling team from the Olympics for life. Then I began to get very angry. My GP kindly offered medication to help me through it but I declined, opting instead for blitz cleaning one room after another, but still I was highly troubled. Then, with the help of a bottle of vintage port followed by three days of weeping I cleansed myself. I would not recommend this as the most sensible remedy but it worked. Soon I began to put on weight and by the summer, when I was due to be plumbed into the ileo-anal pouch which had been in place since the previous autumn I was over seven stone and gaining. The operation was a success and I was home a week later.

The pouch behaved beautifully and the psychological effect of getting rid of the 'sporran' was wonderful, although it was a strange feeling saying goodbye to 'little Willie', a part of me that I would never see again. I have long since forgotten the despair and indignities of those years and have felt great ever since. I will never forget the kindness and attendance of friends and family but I don't know how I would react if I came face to face with a certain consultant. He may recognise himself in this story.

Chapter 12

The Blair Atholl Years

BACK to 1980, and my journey had taken me to that crossroads without a signpost. My old friend and fellow Heretic John Herdman asked me out to dinner to tell me that he had decided to become a monk. It seemed we had both come to an impasse in our lives. I was sick of responsibility, committees and the city. I said to John that what I really wanted to do was throw the whole thing up and open a bed and breakfast in Perthshire.

The upshot was that we decided we would get married and go and live in Perthshire. We happened to be up in Stornoway looking after my sister's bed and breakfast, and we heard from somebody that a house in Blair Atholl was on the market. It was owned by Iain Mac'Illechiar, and I had stayed there several times when I was singing in the area.

It was a beautiful house and John's mother helped us buy some of the furniture that was already there. It was all Edwardian and I set about adding to its character over the years. Every penny I made on bed and breakfast went into acquiring something more, even finding Edwardian-looking wallpaper and brass beds.

I decided how I was going to approach it, because over the years I had been in so many B&Bs while travelling with plays, that I knew exactly what *not* to do. So, from the very beginning I set a standard. I had pure bone china for breakfast and I always had a starched white tablecloth and thick paper napkins in blue because the cups were in white with a blue rim. I went to antique shops and sales; it took me years to find a full Greek key patterned dinner service, but I found it eventually. Then for dinner I had a polished table with crystal and silver and starched napkins.

I always served fresh produce, as local as possible. Angus the butcher was at the top of the lane and provided my freshly cut bacon and sausages every morning. That saved me buying bulk and it going to waste, because I always knew the night before what people wanted for breakfast and just got what I needed. I've never been able to find bacon like it since.

That was the standard I set. One year when I was coming back from Atholl Highland Games on the last weekend in May, I caught up with the MacFarlanes, who had just moved in two doors down. We walked home together and I asked Katie if she'd like to help me. "Oh yes," she said, "I'm bored stiff." So Katie started assisting me in the house. We would go upstairs together after breakfast and strip the beds, then I would leave her upstairs. But the fun we had! She had been a housekeeper in 'the big hoose' for Colonel Haig and the Colman's Mustard people, and she had so many stories about the visitors, their eccentricities and how mean most of them were.

We had great, great fun, and developed a fantastic friendship. Her husband, Donald, had spent all his years on the hill as a gamekeeper, and he was fed up with the tiny little garden they had, so he started tending half of my garden. I did the raspberries, strawberries, herbs and wildflowers, and he did the tatties, carrots, turnips and cabbage. We ended up dividing the produce and shared rhubarb and lettuce with everybody in the vicinity, so it was really a little commune we had going. It became the closest thing to a community that I'd been in since leaving home in Marvig.

My daughters, Mary and Jane, were independent by that time, but they came up regularly. George and his new wife and family eventually started coming up also. Then John's mother got poorly and I went and looked after her in Edinburgh for a bit. John had gone off to work in Fife, and then he moved out altogether. It just wasn't working, and after his mother died we divorced, but remain really good friends.

I kept on at Woodlands, and then I started getting accolades. I appeared in 'The Good Bed and Breakfast Guide', one of only two B&Bs in Scotland out of the top twenty in the UK, the other being Old Craigmore in Rothesay, but I didn't even know I had been inspected. I was on my way to Edinburgh and had stopped at friends in Kirkliston for a cup of tea. When they said, "Congratulations," I replied, "What are you talking about?" And there it was in the press. Reporters had gone up to Blair Atholl when I was out (I'd been doing something at STV) and the papers were full of it the next day. "Mrs Herdman", they called me, but nobody realised that it was Dolina Maclennan, the folksinger-actress, which was great, because they would have made even more of a fuss over it.

As it was, it generated tremendous business. 'The Good Bed and Breakfast Guide' was edited by Elsie Dillard and Susan Causin. It was Susan who came to see me and we became very good friends, but at the time I didn't know she'd been; they don't tell you. They said, 'Woodlands. This little house in its own garden is in a peaceful spot on the edge of Blair Atholl ... and its views of the hills. Dolina Maclennan has made her mark in the charming and imaginative decoration and furnishing. Her time is split between bed and breakfast and an acting career, mostly in Gaelic language television ... She is also a keen cook and guests can be assured of excellent Highland hospitality ...'

Then there was Alastair Sawday's 'Special Places to Stay in Britain': 'Doli is wonderful ... A well-known Gaelic singer and storyteller, she loves her old house too much to vandalise it by putting in ensuites ... no telly or plastic trays in bedrooms either ... Just nice old furniture, brass beds, creaking floorboards and some most excitable plumbing. Cooking superb – all local, all Scottish, jugged kippers, smoked haddock and home-baked bread for breakfast. No wonder people are entranced and come back again and again.'

One article in *The Scotsman* in November 2004 began: 'Walking into Dolina Maclennan's home fresh from the city is like taking a step off the treadmill. A pot of home-made soup simmers on the stove in the kitchen, while the inviting crackle of an open fire can be heard from the living room. William Morris wallpaper adorns the walls of the enticing hallway, creating a rich entrance to each room in this Edwardian house.'

Peter Irvine mentioned me in 'Scotland the Best': 'book in at Dolina Maclennan's B&B if you're lucky enough to get in' and Derek Cooper, the food writer, gave me so many write ups. He and his wife called in one day on their way to Skye, and because it was lunchtime and we only had an hour, we didn't move into the dining room but I made kedgeree and we just sat in the kitchen and had it with home-made bread. He wrote a long article about it the next week, saying that he could still taste the kedgeree when he arrived in Skye. He meant it as a compliment, but I didn't know quite how to take that!

Another good report read: 'Bannocks at dawn. Miss Dolina Maclennan plays Ishbel in *Machair* and Flora in *Hamish MacBeth*. She also does television cooking, writes and does storytelling and, as she tells Leilah Farrah, she runs bed and breakfast at her home in Blair Atholl.'

I remember Leilah Farrar, who was a freelance writer, came to stay during the annual Glenfiddich Piping Championships at Blair Castle. There were two great weekends in the year, the horse trials (they came later, a three-day event) and the Glenfiddich piping championship. I'd had the same crowd from Lewis for the Glenfiddich for fourteen years; John Smith who was a doctor in Carloway and his wife Muriel, John Kennedy and yet another John (MacDonald) who was a farmer outside Inverness. Those three, with partners or sons or daughters, as many as I could squeeze in, would arrive for the Glenfiddich, and quite often Simon Mackenzie (the actor and Gaelic theatre activist) would come as well. I'd always have a haunch of venison marinating in claret, vegetables and herbs for five days, turning it once a day. They'd arrive on the Friday night and as they came out of the car and up to the door John Kennedy would play *Crossing the Minch* on his set of electric pipes.

Another great night was the Aberfeldy Ball in Blair Castle during the first weekend in December. Again, the same people came for that for years. They were all lawyers and their wives, with connections to Aberfeldy. They would arrive on the Friday afternoon and I would make dozens of pancakes, pots of tea and home-made jam. They would just sit round the fire in the sitting room and chat, because some of them only ever actually met up at that time as they were all living in different parts of Scotland. Then they would go upstairs to change, but they'd say, "Och, I don't want to go to the ball. I just want to stay here." But they would go up and get into their kilts and evening frocks and when they came back down I'd give them a dram or a glass of sherry and off they'd go to the ball.

I'd make a big pot of soup and leave it on the Aga and when they came back, about four o'clock in the morning, they would help themselves in the kitchen. I just charged them for bed and breakfast (about fifteen pounds) and that was that. I enjoyed doing it so much that making money out of it wasn't important. I didn't pay myself either, and usually if there was anything left over it went on the car, or on something for the house. I was actually in debt when I left, but I don't regret a minute of it.

There was nothing stolen from the house during all those years, not even a towel. There were bits of silver and porcelain and all sorts of ornaments and books in all the rooms and pretty things on the dressing tables, but nothing was ever taken. I suppose it was because people treated it as their own home rather than somewhere to visit.

Some guests had all sorts of eccentricities, though. There was the guy who came with his teddy bears. He would bring one down to breakfast and it had to have its own chair and place setting. Then there was the German who, when I asked him to sign the book, just took out a rubber stamp and ink pad from his pocket and *stamped* it like that, with his name and address. It stuck out like a sore thumb in among all the gushing remarks from the other guests.

I think had a narrow escape on one occasion. A couple came from Northern Ireland, and the husband looked very like Ian Paisley. He was a huge guy, and he was weird; you could tell he was a bully, because his wife was very cowed and even stirred his tea for him. And I don't know how it came about but he pulled up his sleeve and said, "Look at that," and he had the red hand of Ulster tattooed on it. He was an older man, and he just gave me the grue. They asked if they could stay another night but I said, "I'm sorry, booked out." I did have room but I just couldn't bear him in the house.

In fact, the next night I didn't have anybody, but about half past ten the doorbell rang and there was a young man, by himself and absolutely dripping wet, who said, "I just saw your light on. Have you got accommodation?" I said, "Yes, come in. You're soaking." He looked okay and I gave him something hot. And we were sitting by the fire and I asked him what he did, and he said, "I'm a priest from Ireland." He'd been camping in Glen Tilt but the heavens had opened and he had come to the nearest light he saw. We had such fun, and I said to him, "Your God worked very hard this morning because he got me to get rid of the creep who was here last night."

Then there was the American woman I met when I was lecturing at the summer school at the Geneva Point Centre in New Hampshire. While I was there, someone took me to a huge retail strip at Conway where we parked next to a car which had an "I ♥ Scotland" sticker on the window. I put my Woodlands Guest House card on her windscreen, and that was that.

However, after I got back to Blair Atholl, I got a letter from her. Her name was Priscilla Fairweather. I wrote back and the following year we met and spent a day together in New Hampshire. She was the most delightful lady, and it turned out that her folks came from Habost, which is eight miles from Marvig. She discovered this through meeting me, and we used to keep in touch by phone and write.

She was terribly on my mind one night. I couldn't stop thinking of her, so I phoned her in America from Woodlands. It was her daughter who answered, and she said, "My mother has just passed away." I was so distressed, because I was going to invite her over and take her home to Habost.

The daughter said she was coming over, and in due course she and a man arrived at Woodlands one night. She seemed very nice and we had a chat, had supper and I said, "I'm so, so sorry that your mother never made it to Scotland." And she said, "Oh but she has." She took a little bag out and it was her mother's ashes. We put some under both my rowan trees, and they've been beautiful ever since.

క్ర

People used to refer to the 'Tarmacs', and I thought it was some species of bird, until I heard someone say, "Aye, the third yin's no' her own. She fell in wi' a Tarmac." Then I had the 'Tarmacs' staying myself; not those responsible for the above situation, I hasten to add. They were the road builders, working on the A9 at Killiecrankie. They were Geordies; a father and two sons, and they were lovely, lovely people, though I had to tell so many lies on their behalf, because their wives would phone up every night to speak to them and I'd say, "Oh, they're working late," when they'd be off in the pub.

They had a packed lunch every day, and they called it their "bait". Butter was "budda", so I learned a lot from that crowd. They didn't like the Tilt Hotel for some reason. So if there was any naughtiness going on, I'd say, "Listen, you'll be back to the Tilt Hotel next week if this goes on." But one night I was the one out late, over at my friend Chrissie's, and they locked the door, thinking I was already in my bed. I started throwing stones up at the window of one of the boys. I shouted, "You've locked me out," and he said, "If this happens again you're going to be back in the Tilt."

It was hard, hard work. I had to get up at six in the morning to see them off, but at least I didn't have the six, eight, twelve sheets to change every day, which I would have if I just had guests for a night or two.

⚬

One morning the phone rang and a voice asked if it was me. I said yes, then it said, "This is Ruby Wax." I said, "Oh yes, pull the other one," and she explained that she was doing a series called 'Wax on Wheels', in which she went everywhere in a coach. She said, "I'm coming up to the highlands, could you put me up? And could you introduce me to some interesting people." Tom McGrath, the playwright, had put her in touch with me; she was a good friend of Tom's from when she was at drama college in Glasgow.

I just had twenty-four hours to find some interesting characters for her. Fortunately I was surrounded by them, so I went up to the pub and found some folk there who promised to come down. So I had a houseful for the next night when Ruby and her producer duly arrived. She certainly met a lot of interesting people, but then she got round to telling me that she really wanted to meet a big Highlander. I phoned the storyteller Paraig MacNeil, who wears the old belted plaid, and he was all for it.

When it came to do the actual filming, the cameras were trained on the house as Ruby arrived; it was the best publicity Woodlands could have got. She came in and sat at the kitchen table and asked what Highlanders were like, were they romantic and so on, all the usual nonsense. I sang her a song and she said she wanted to go up to bed. I had a big flannelette nightdress my mother used to have so I gave her that and a candle and she went up to the small room upstairs. This one had a lovely brass bed and when she opened the door, there was Paraig sitting on the bed, waiting for her, with his plaid over his shoulder. So she found her Heilan' man. All good clean fun.

Among the other personalities who stayed in the house was Valerie Singleton, best known as the presenter of 'Blue Peter'. She first came to Blair Atholl to do a story on the Loch Garry Tree Group, a local tree planting initiative. *The Sunday Times* and Radio 4's 'PM' programme got together to find the best conservation project in the British Isles. They had thousands of entries, the Loch Garry Tree Group being one of them. I remember when they came to look at it I had been decorating; there was no carpet on the stairs or anything, and who should arrive but Valerie, who was presenting 'PM' at that time, and two men from *The Times*. They went out to Loch Garry on one of the worst days; it was a blizzard out there. When they came back and I gave them hot soup and baked bread. They didn't stay that time, but Valerie had to go upstairs; up that uncarpeted stair. But she just loved the house. The Loch Garry Tree Group eventually won the prize (£5,000) by public vote. After that, Valerie came to stay with me quite a lot and we're still in touch.

I also had the pleasure of playing host to the first Dutchman to climb every Munro. Johann de Jong was a guest for many years and became a dear friend. He and his lady friend even came over for my 60th birthday.

I enjoyed many visits from MacDuff Everton, the famous photographer and his wife, Mary Heebner, the well-known artist from Santa Barbara. The last time he was over he was doing a series of whisky images for Bill Gates.

All those fascinating people came to stay, including the Norwegian consul and his wife, who brought the Austrian consul and his wife. Ron Greer, the freshwater biologist, ecologist and forestry expert, would take them out. They just loved coming up because they enjoyed getting away from the pretentiousness of Edinburgh they said. They would come back from fishing about ten o'clock at night and sit down to dinner. I remember at half-past midnight one evening I went into the dining room, sat in a corner and started singing a lullaby, by way of a hint. They were ready to sit at the table until two in the morning, but I had to clear up the kitchen and get ready for breakfast.

You never knew who was going to show up. It was such a happy time and I was heartbroken to have to leave it. But after being diagnosed as a coeliac and in spite of the successful operations, I just wasn't well enough to carry on running Woodlands in the style which won it all the commendations.

I was, in a word, broke, despite twenty years of hard work and dedication. The only way I could see my way out was to sell, and to be totally honest, at the time I didn't expect to live for very long. So I sold my beautiful home and bought a flat in Edinburgh. But here I am, eleven years later. On one's life journey, there is no time allowed for 'if only'.

Chapter 13

The Latest Stage in the Journey

M Y INTEREST in politics was stimulated long before I knew what the word meant. I knew before my age was in double figures that Marvig voted Labour and Calbost (two miles away) voted Tory. I have no proof of this and maybe it's a complete myth!

My father was, before his death in 1950, an agent of sorts for Malcolm K Macmillan (Labour MP for the Western Isles, 1935–1970) in the South Lochs area. We had red flags and bunting on the gate on election days. At the 1950 general election I remember my father organising lifts to the polling station in Cromore for the Labour voters while the Tories had to walk on a sheep track across the moor.

I didn't really understand politics as such at eight years old, but I must have absorbed by osmosis the idea of socialism, pacifism and equality, because I never had to consciously learn to embrace them. Obviously I was aware that the minister, the doctor and the dominie were 'better' than the rest of us, but I have a sneaking feeling that father disabused me of that predominant attitude by surreptitious indoctrination when he told me my bedtime stories.

However it wasn't until arriving in Edinburgh in the late 1950s that I came across real snobbery. Which school did you go to? What does your Daddy do? Where do you shoot and fish? My replies were simple: we shoot usually in the '*Ard Fhalasger*' (a moorland peninsula near the village, the haunt of ducks and cormorants) and we fish in the Minch.

It was at that time that I was introduced to the notion of Scottish nationalism. I met old timers like Wendy Wood, George Nicholson, Jimmy Glendinning and the wonderful Willie Kellock who organised the famous Bo'ness Rebel Ceilidhs, at which yours truly was a frequent participant, and I mustn't forget the wonderful Angus MacGillivray, who was a tireless fund-raiser for the party.

I still voted Labour at that time because the SNP was a bit of a joke among the majority of people – as were folk singers! I remember, around 1958 or '59, seven or eight men sounding off on the Mound on a Sunday evening about English rule, and passers-by laughing at them. I remembered them and shed a tear for them on the Saturday in September 2012 when ten thousand marched from the Meadows to Princes Street Gardens to show their support for an independent Scotland.

As time went on I became more and more enamoured of the nationalist movement and while performing with 7:84 Theatre Company at the Abbey Theatre in Dublin in 1974 I got the answer I was seeking. A gentleman came up to me after one of the performances of 'The Cheviot, The Stag and The Black, Black Oil' and said, "What a nationalist you must be."

I replied that I was a patriot, and that I couldn't equate nationalism with socialism. This man, whose name I never knew, replied, "Remember what James Connolly said." I asked him what in particular and he told me, "A nation first of all has to be free to make its own decisions."

So on the 4th of July 1974, I went to the SNP's then HQ in Manor Place and joined the party. I'm afraid that John McGrath found it necessary to mention in a foreword to one of his books that I had joined the SNP, as if one couldn't still be a socialist and believe in the freedom of one's country. I called myself a 'Red Nat', but now I'm glad to say that, if anything, I'd call myself a 'Green Nat', because the Labour party that my father and his ilk fought for no longer exists.

I was also involved over the years with the Scotland-USSR Society, Amnesty International and the Chile Solidarity Campaign. Throughout elections Woodlands became the focal point for local canvassing. I have memories of coffee, soup, pancakes, and that amazing 'high' of anticipation. Ron Greer, a local activist, and I would go to all the outlying farms. I would drive and Ron would approach the farmsteads, sometimes to shouts of, "it's you two b------s again, come in for a dram."

I remember when the late and much lamented Allan Macartney won the Euro election for North-East Scotland in 1994. A crowd of us, including the late John Cullins and SNP councillor Eleanor Howie, met in the car park behind Fisher's Hotel in Pitlochry. We had a radio and were waiting for the results to be announced. An almighty cheer went up when the news came. I ran to the off-sales and said to the astonished man behind the counter, "Two bottles of champagne and a dozen glasses." He handed over the lot without question, whereupon we had a pop-up street party with passers-by joining in. I remember singing mouth music for a strip-the-willow.

It was very exciting living in Perthshire during the last part of the 20th century. First to fall was Perth & Kinross when Roseanna Cunningham took the 'safe' Tory seat left by the death of Nicholas Fairbairn. Then John Swinney won Tayside North, and when Pete Wishart took his Westminster seat for North Tayside that was the icing on the cake.

When I moved back to Edinburgh due to circumstances already explained, I joined the Edinburgh branch of the SNP and have been active ever since. I was honoured last year by the branch and was made an honorary life member. Now Edinburgh Central, it has the largest membership in the country and, I believe, one of the most politically active.

The count after the 2011 election was nothing short of electrifying. I and many others had been working non-stop for the campaign, manning the office, driving our candidate, feeding our gallant young workers and being generally handy. One story bears telling; it has, needless to say, been 'embroidered' with the passing of time. It was 2.30am on the morning after the royal wedding. Edinburgh Council would not allow us to put posters up on lampposts until after midnight on the 29th of April so at the witching hour I set off in my car, with a ladder, to pick up a couple of stalwarts at the SNP club and we proceeded to plaster all the lampposts in Slateford and Gorgie.

Having finished our beat, I drove Alasdair home to Bruntsfield and proceeded to take young Liam back to his parents' home at the foot of Ferry Road. We were almost there and I was driving at about ten miles an hour, not knowing exactly where his parents lived. Next thing a flashing police car appeared behind me and, like the good citizen, I drew into the side to let them pass. Not a bit of it; it was me they were after. A big burly polisman approached and I opened my door and asked if I was doing anything wrong. Your man was visibly startled, and when he was joined by his WPC they looked at each other and couldn't hide their amusement. The last thing they expected to find was a white-haired old lady with painted fingernails. Yes, that was the night I was stopped for kerb crawling.

On the morning of the election a young German politics student called Tilo, who had been a great help throughout the campaign, came to breakfast at 6am. The two of us proceeded to put out the A-Boards at all the polling stations in the New Town and Stockbridge. We took them in at the same time the following morning, not having slept for twenty-four hours.

I wept profusely that night at the count, as the results kept coming in with yet another SNP win. When about 5.15am our own Marco Biagi was declared as the winning candidate for Edinburgh Central, it meant more than is possible to explain in words.

అ

There have been so many significant episodes on my journey, but one particular off-the-cuff comment altered the future lives of many people. It happened on a sunny Saturday morning in 1997, when my old friend David Campbell, then a BBC radio producer, arrived at Woodlands on his way to climb a Perthshire hill. I was polishing a brass bed (strange how some details remain so vivid) and as David left his bag before setting off for the hill, he told me a strange story about meeting an old friend in the street, who asked him if he fancied going to America for four weeks all expenses paid. Apparently the people who had been booked to go couldn't make it and were anxiously looking for stand-ins.

After explaining this to me, David said, "I have to bring a woman." To which I replied, "When do we go?" "Friday," was the response and we both burst out laughing. But we decided to find out more. The couple, John Clifford and his wife Eliza, were due to go and give a series of lectures in New Hampshire at a place called Geneva Point Centre on Lake Winnipesaukee but had had to call off at the last minute. They had told David's friend to ask around, and by happenstance he met David, who by chance was visiting Blair Atholl the next day.

Well, by the end of the week, having sorted out passports, visas and other travel arrangements, and with much trepidation, we were on our way to ... where? We had no idea; it was the first time either of us had been to the United States. The only thing we knew was that we had to give a series of talks about Scotland to groups of fifty elderly people for four weeks (we had the third week off to travel, car provided).

After a complicated journey we landed at Newark instead of Boston (I can't remember why) and were met by a lovely, blonde, handsome young lady called Linda Bandelier, who turned out to be a Methodist minister from Montana. She drove us through New England in the autumn sunshine to an idyllic spot miles from anywhere, and introduced us to our home for the next month – two hundred lakeside acres of log cabins and meeting rooms.

Geneva Point Centre (GPC) caters for visiting groups of people throughout the summer months. Our group, in Elder Hostel, were over-sixties who were there to have their special interests in Scotland, its folklore and culture, catered for. Fifty people would arrive on the Sunday evening and David and I each had to lecture to them for ninety minutes each day until they left the following Friday. Then another fifty would arrive, and so on.

Back home, in the meantime, the Atholl Highlanders (the Duke of Atholl's private army) were also preparing to cross the Atlantic, for Loon Mountain Highland Games. I used to tease Alex Barbour, the Duke's factor, saying that they ought to have a real Gaelic speaker with them for these trips. Not having any detailed idea of American geography, we were highly amused to discover that Loon Mountain was just up the road from GPC, so you can imagine the surprise of my friends from the village when I turned up. I'll never forget the sight of the Atholl Highlanders, led by Iain Murray, the then Duke of Atholl, marching on to the arena in front of five thousand spectators.

That was the first of five annual visits by me to GPC. The first life-changing event was when Linda Bandelier came to Edinburgh and she and David were married at the top of Arthur's Seat, on Christmas Eve's morning, complete with minister and Norman Chalmers accompanying the hymns on his squeezebox.

It was on one of these trips that I met the lovely Priscilla Fairweather, already mentioned, whose ashes are now under the rowan tree at Woodlands.

In 1990 my daughter Jane decided to begin her world tour by volunteering at the centre, before moving on to Canada and regions beyond. That was until she met Trevor Bechtel and fell in love. The saga that followed is their journey. Suffice to say that Trevor moved to Scotland, where they were married by none other than the same Linda Bandelier. They presented me with the most wonderful two grandchildren, Catriona and Annie, who are now, in 2014, twenty-three and twenty respectively and both attending universities. Trevor's parents are regular visitors, as are many other people whom I met on that stretch of my journey.

So from that "When do we go?" throw-away comment came all those amazing happenings.

I have travelled to Mexico a few times to visit the family of Robin Gray, my old folk-singing partner, who married a Mexican plastic surgeon and who died many years ago. I'm introduced by his daughters as, "Daddy's first girlfriend". Alicia, his widow, still a plastic surgeon, always wants to do things to my face, "a leetle tuck here and a leetle tuck there", but so far I have renaged. I have grown into my wrinkles.

In spite of, or maybe because of, the magical allure of those exotic places, I realised from the start that I could never leave my beloved Scotland.

CR

Every journey has its pitfalls, its high and lows, and I have had my share of both. Losing so many family and friends is heartbreaking, but was I not fortunate in having them in my life in the first place? I'm so lucky in having my two ex-husbands, George and John, and their respective wives, as my friends. I have my lovely daughters, Mary and Jane, and their spouses; Rory a big, handsome Irishman, and Trevor, whom I have described already; my granddaughters Catriona and Annie; my American in-laws and so many caring friends.

Stuart MacGregor once wrote, 'Memory's a rogue / that jetisons what's bleak / I'm sure we used to sing / where now we speak.' Nevertheless, the singing and the music, the laughter and the love, is what I remember, and I shall sing and dance and laugh and love, especially if I live to see my country free.

*Dolina received the Fletcher of Saltoun Award from
the Saltire Society in 2012 for her significant contribution to
Scotland's life and culture*